Helping the Injured or Disabled Member:

A Guidebook for the Washington Law Enforcement and Fire Union Representative

Jim Cline and Erica Shelley Nelson

ISBN-13: 978-0-9967645-3-7

TABLE OF CONTENTS

FOREWORD

When a public safety employee suffers an injury or otherwise develops a medical condition which impedes his or her ability to do ordinary duties, the stakes are raised. A very livelihood is threatened. Especially for those employees in physically arduous occupations like commissioned law enforcement, corrections, or firefighting, such limitations may ultimately result in the loss of a career. In this Book, we address what legal protections injured and disabled employees have in this process, both in the short-term and in the long-term.

The legal environment for law enforcement officers and firefighters is simply different than for other professions. While there are various state and federal laws that apply to all types of employees, there are many special rules and programs that apply *only* to law enforcement and firefighters. It is important that a police or fire union leader understand both the general rules and the special rules. While many of the rights described here belong to the individual officers and firefighters, you, as an effective union representative will want to be fully versed in what rights your members have both under the law and how those rights relate to the Collective Bargaining Agreement.

Some rights you can directly assert as the Collective Bargaining Representative. Other rights are simply beyond the enforcement powers of the union itself. But even in those cases, by fully informing yourself of the universe of rights and the limitations on those rights, you can provide extremely useful assistance to your members at a critical time in which they most need it. For these reasons, we decided to write down, all in a single book, all the points concerning representing the injured or disabled member that we thought you would want to know.

Some of the principles here are straightforward and common sense. Many are complex and often involve an interplay between connected (and disconnected) statutory and contractual rights. Many of the rights identified here you will be able to directly enforce as a union officer under your CBA. Some rights are individual in nature and can only be enforced by the affected member in court or before an administrative agency. To make matters more complicated, some of the individual rights are "implied" into your CBA and can be enforced through the grievance procedure.

Armed with the knowledge in this book, you should be able to protect the rights of your members through direct action and member advice. On the other hand, many of the issues that arise here will require the involvement and counsel of the union attorney or other civil lawyers.

This book covers the rights of your injured or disabled members under the ADA, WLAD, FMLA, PDA, IIA, WISHA, LEOFF Supplement, Social Security, PSOBA, and your CBA. We will work to simplify this "alphabet soup" of statutes. But we have to acknowledge that it is not always possible to provide a simple answer in all circumstances because of the sometimes complex manner in which there is "interplay" among these laws.

In the end, we hope you have a practical set of guidelines to follow and resources to turn to in order to help your members. We want to give you a "tool bag" with all the tools that you need in every situation that might realistically arise. At the time they face injury or disqualifying disability, they are most in need of the best possible advice. Our goal is to assist you in getting that advice to them.

Chapter 1: The Right to a Reasonable Accommodation: State and Federal Disability Discrimination Laws

A. Introduction

This chapter covers disability discrimination laws which apply to employees who are limited in their ability to work due to injury or disability. It includes a discussion of state and federal disability discrimination laws. We also address how these laws relate to the *separate* employer obligation to engage in collective bargaining. Most of the laws here are "individual" in nature, in that they extend legal rights to your members separate and apart from the CBA. On the other hand, though, many of these mandates effectively become integrated into your CBA, either through express cross-referencing (for example a clause that says the employer will follow the ADA or the FMLA) or through the application of more general legal clauses such as "just cause" or nondiscrimination.

One of the main points to be stressed as we cover these competing laws is that you cannot just examine a single statute and have the answer for an individual's situation. In most disability situations, more than one law applies and the employer, of course, must comply with all the laws. The myriad of laws may seem somewhat conflicting, but they can be "harmonized" and, in fact, must be.

The net result is that when these issues arise you will likely want some early and immediate "hands on" assistance of your legal counsel. And often your member too may need to retain their own private counsel, especially since their interests and the union's interests may diverge and because they have rights that surpass those simply available in the CBA.

There are potential traps for all concerned, but if everyone involved entered this process in good faith and with the goal of being reasonable, the best possible outcome can be achieved. There is an overall duty of "reasonable accommodation" and that's what we turn to next.

B. State and Federal Disability Discrimination Laws

1. General Obligations of Employers

Applicable Statutes. Attention has been paid by public safety employers, and unions as well, to the Americans with Disabilities Act (ADA). But the focus on the ADA has often been misplaced. There are *three different* disability discrimination statutes which apply to Washington public safety employers, and, in some respects, the ADA is the least stringent of these three.

The ADA was preceded by another federal law, the Rehabilitation Act of 1973.[1] The Rehabilitation Act prohibits discrimination against disabled persons by federal agencies and all entities receiving federal financial assistance.[2] The ADA broadened the coverage against discrimination to reach most employers, private and public.[3]

Most local governments in Washington are subject to the Rehabilitation Act because they need only receive a nominal amount of federal assistance in order to qualify for the Act's jurisdictional requirements. Separately, Washington State law RCW 49.60.180 also prohibits discrimination against persons with disabilities.

The state law, as we will discuss below, takes a *more expansive* view of what constitutes a "disability."

Differences between Statutes. The ADA followed the pattern set forth by the Rehabilitation Act, but it did not totally supplant it. There are some differences between the two statutes and there are circumstances where each offers greater protections to employees than the other statute. Employers must comply with the requirements of both. Most of these differences are technical and do not immediately impact your role as a union representative; you just want to be aware that there are various statutes and to recognize that a court interpretation under one law does not necessarily extend to the other laws.

---

[1] 29 U.S.C. § 790, *et seq.*
[2] 29 U.S.C. § 794(a).
[3] 42 U.S.C. § 12111.

For those of us involved in Washington labor and employment issues, this point is especially important to remember. The state law, as we will discuss below, takes a *more expansive* view of what constitutes a "disability." Having a qualifying "disability" is what opens the door to the protection of these disabilities statutes. The Washington Law against Discrimination (WLAD) also often, depending on the issue, imposes a higher standard on employers as to the extent of accommodation owed.

The differences between the ADA and the Rehabilitation Act are relatively minor, at least relative to the difference between the federal laws and the state law. By and large, in enacting the ADA, Congress adopted the statutory structure that had been set forth under the Rehabilitation Act. As a result, when the ADA was adopted, federal courts looked at prior Rehabilitation Act cases to help guide their interpretation of the ADA.

Elements of the ADA. It is important to understand first the narrow, carefully crafted language of the statute. First, the statute prohibits discrimination, in a number of forms, against individuals with "disabilities." The statute defines "disability" as a: "(a) a physical or mental impairment that substantially limits one or more of the major life activities of such individual; (b) a record of such an impairment; or (c) being regarded as having such an impairment."[4]

Therefore, an employee need not have an actual current medical limitation to be considered disabled. It is enough that the employee either has had that condition in the past, or that he is *perceived* as having one by an employer. The "perception" element becomes important when the employer discriminates based on stereotypical perceptions of what persons who have had certain disabilities in the past are capable of.

The general statement of prohibition of discrimination under the ADA is that

> [N]o covered entity shall discriminate against a qualified individual with a disability because of the disability if such individual in regard to job application procedures, the hiring, advancement, or discharge of employees, employee compensation, job training, and other terms, conditions and privileges of employment.[5]

---

[4] 42 U.S.C. § 12102(2).
[5] 42 U.S.C. § 12112(a).

Therefore, to be entitled to the protection under the ADA, an employee *must* be a “qualified individual with a disability.”

The statute also defines a “qualified individual with a disability”:

> The term qualified individual with a disability means an individual with a disability who, with or without reasonable accommodation, can perform the essential functions of the employment position that such individual holds or desires. For purposes of this title, consideration shall be given to the employer’s judgment as to what functions of a job are essential, and if an employer has prepared a written job description before advertising or interviewing applicants for the job, the description shall be considered evidence of the essential functions of the job.[6]

Therefore, to be a qualified individual with a disability entitled to protection from the statute, the employee must have:

- A disability; and
- The ability to perform the “essential functions” of the job — with or without a “reasonable accommodation.”

Only after employees can demonstrate that they meet this rigorous standard, can they invoke the protections of the ADA. In other words, if they cannot prove that they are qualified individuals with a handicap (or are “perceived” as such) *they have no protection against discrimination under this law.* But if they can meet this test, then they can assert an entitlement to a “reasonable accommodation” of their disability.

The ADA defines “reasonable accommodation”:

[6] 42 U.S.C. § 12111(8).

> The term reasonable accommodation may include (a) making facilities used by employees readily accessible to and usable by individuals with disabilities and (b) job restructuring, part-time or modified work schedules, reassignment to a vacant position, acquisition or modification of equipment or devices, appropriate adjustment or modification of examinations, training materials or policies, the provision of qualified readers or interpreters, and other similar accommodations for individuals with disabilities.[7]

These are the types of accommodations an employer *may* make. But even these identified accommodations are *not* mandated *if* they would not be "reasonable" (as that term is elsewhere defined in the law).[8] That exit door exists due to the "undue burden" test and other related defenses.

The statute defines a reasonable accommodation as one that does not impose "an undue hardship on the operation of the business of such covered entities."[9] In adopting the ADA, Congress defined "undue hardship" as "an action requiring significant difficulty or expense."[10]

Congress identified a number of factors to consider in assessing whether an accommodation involved an undue hardship. The primary factor is "the nature and cost of the accommodation needed."[11] But the nature and cost of accommodation is to be balanced against the "overall financial resources of the 'facility' involved and the 'covered entities.' "[12] It also allows consideration of "the type of operation or operations of the covered entity, including the composition, structure and functions of the workforce of such entity."[13]

---

[7] 42 U.S.C. § 12111(9).
[8] 42 U.S.C. § 12111 (5)(a).
[9] 42 U.S.C. § 12112(5)(b).
[10] 42 U.S.C. § 12111(10).
[11] *Id.*
[12] *Id.*
[13] *Id.*

There are two major areas where employees lose their coverage of the ADA. First, there is a requirement that the condition "substantially limits one or more of the major life activities of such individual."[14] Although "work" is listed as a major life activity, there is a dispute among the courts about whether work means one particular job, a class of jobs, or the ability to work in general. For example, the courts are split on the question of whether the inability of an employee to work as a police officer or firefighter substantially limits a "major life activity" where an individual can do other work, even within the same department.

The second area where employees lose out on ADA coverage is the "essential functions" requirement. If an employee cannot fulfill the *bona fide* "essential functions" of the position — with or without reasonable accommodation — the individual is not covered under the discrimination protections of the ADA. Often, three leading issues that arise in connection with fulfilling essential functions are:

- Whether the functions claimed as necessary by the employer are truly "essential."
- Whether the employee can perform those functions with or without an accommodation.
- If an individual who could perform the "essential functions" only with accommodation, whether that accommodation is a "reasonable" one.

Elements of Washington Law. For reasons discussed below, the Washington law grants employees broader coverage and is almost always the law selected in preference to the federal law when plaintiffs litigate their disability claims. Primarily this is due to a much broader definition of the term "disability."

Washington law grants employees broader coverage and is almost always the law selected in preference to the federal law when plaintiffs litigate their disability claims. Primarily this is due to a much broader definition of the term "disability."

[14] 42 U.S.C. § 12102(1).

The Washington state disability discrimination law (WLAD), like the ADA, starts by making it unlawful to discriminate against individuals based on their "disability." But, oddly, the statute itself does not specifically define "disability." Rather it defines "disability" in almost the most general of terms to mean:

> [T]he presence of a sensory, mental, or physical, impairment that: Is medically cognizable or diagnosable; or exists as a record or history; or is perceived to exist whether or not it exists in fact." [15]

To supplement this broad concept of "disability" as simply a "diagnosable" medical "impairment," the law is further clarified by the regulations of the Human Rights Commission. But these regulations still define disability in broad terms. The regulations refer to disability as involving simply a health condition with an "abnormality,"[16] which only slightly narrows the definition of "disability." Unlike the ADA, the WLAD does *not* require that to be qualifying the disability must affect a "major life activity." *This difference is key and is why the state disability law offers much greater protection, in most cases, than the federal laws.*

Even though this broad definition of disability might seem to create almost boundless claims of protection, courts have somewhat reigned in the scope of the statute by incorporating some of the federal law concepts. Specifically, and importantly, the courts have redefined "reasonable accommodation" to *exclude* accommodations which involve maintaining employees in a position for which they cannot perform the "essential functions" of the job.[17]

There are some differences and similarities in how the federal laws and the state law approach the concept of "reasonable accommodation." Both sets of laws agree that an accommodation is not reasonable if it imposes an undue hardship upon the employer. *The primary difference between state and federal law concerns the accommodation of an individual who cannot fulfill the job functions.*

---

[15] RCW 49.60.040.
[16] *See* WAC 162-22-040.
[17] *See, e.g.*, *Dedman v. Personnel Appeals Board*, 98 Wn. App. 471, 989 P.2d 1214 (1999).

Under the federal laws, if individuals cannot perform the essential functions — with or without reasonable accommodation — they are not entitled to the protection of the disability discrimination portions of the statutes. The state cases, though, have been explicit that even if individuals are unable to perform the essential functions of the job, they are still entitled to protection.

But this liberal protection does not confer on the employee the right to maintain their position. Rather, it obligates the employer to engage in a specific "interactive" process with the employee concerning their availability for alternative positions. In fact, it actually requires the employer to provide *priority consideration* to those individuals for those positions.

Federal cases have been less clear concerning the obligation of employers to accommodate such individuals. A number of cases have held that since the individuals cannot fulfill the essential functions of the job, they are entitled to *no* protection under the statute. But other more recent cases are tending toward the position that there is still an obligation to make a "reasonable accommodation," even with individuals unable to fulfill the job requirements, *and* employers have been held to the obligation to undertake work reassignments to accommodate an individual.

These later decisions explain that since the statute specifically mentions reassignments and job restructuring as a means of making an accommodation, whenever it is possible to assign an employee into a different assignment, that person meets the definition of a "qualified individual" and should, therefore, be accommodated into that different assignment. This more expansive application of the ADA term "qualified individual" would, in these circumstances, grant the individual some protections similar to what is otherwise available under the more liberal WLAD provisions. Regardless, for a variety of reasons mentioned, plaintiffs' employment lawyers virtually always proceed primarily under the WLAD with the ADA no more than an afterthought.

2. Specific Types of Discrimination Issues

Understanding the nature of the accommodation due is often a fact specific inquiry. The Appendix at the end of this Book identifies a wide range of circumstances in which public safety employees have sought an accommodation and what the responses of the courts have been to those requests. The question of whether an accommodation is a "reasonable" one is dependent on a variety of factors. The discussion below also addresses generally how courts have viewed the duty to accommodate in particular situations.

a. Obligation to Create Light Duty Positions

First, the federal laws, at least, do not protect individuals with temporary medical conditions. The right to "light duty" under these circumstances is left to the parties' collective bargaining arrangement (or their established "past practices"). PERC has ruled in *City of Wenatchee* that light duty is a mandatory subject of bargaining and that an employer may not unilaterally abandon a light duty program.[18] (This is another example of the important ways in which collective bargaining rights relate to disability rights.)

The federal cases have been, for the most part, fairly clear that there is *no* obligation to create a permanent light duty program. The basic rule concerning "light duty" accommodation, is stated by the EEOC:

---

[18] *City of Wenatchee*, Decision 6517-A (PECB, 1999)

> The ADA does not require an employer to create a "light duty" position unless the "heavy duty" tasks an injured worker can no longer perform are marginal job functions which may be reallocated to co-workers as part of the reasonable accommodation of job-restructuring. In most cases, however, "light duty" positions involve a totally different job from the job that a worker performed before the injury. *Creating such positions by job restructuring is not required by the ADA.* However, if an employer already has a vacant light duty position for which an injured worker is qualified, it might be a reasonable accommodation to reassign the worker to that position. *If the position was created as a temporary job, a reassignment to that position need only be for a temporary period.*[19]

In the Ninth Circuit, as in other federal circuits, the "reasonableness" of an accommodation will depend on particular circumstances of each case.[20] But here are the general principles that federal courts have applied:

- The ADA *might* require employers to reassign a disabled employee to a different position as a reasonable accommodation when the employee can no longer perform the essential functions of his or her current position;[21]
- On the other hand, employers are *not* required to transform temporary light duty jobs into permanent jobs in order to accommodate a disability;[22]
- Employers are *not* required to create new jobs;[23]
- Employers are *not* bound by earlier "good faith" accommodations of disabled employees;[24] *but* employers probably will be bound where such accommodations are part of an existing policy;[25]

---

[19] EEOC Technical Assistance on Title 1 of ADA 8 FEP Manual (BNA) § 9.4 at 405:7057-58 (1992).

[20] *See Lujan v. Pacific Maritime Association*, 165 F.3d 738 (9th Cir. 1999); *Barnett v. U.S. Air Inc*, 196 F.3d 979 (9th Cir. 1998).

[21] *Malabarba v. Chicago Tribune Co.*, 149 F.3d 690 (7th Cir. 1998).

[22] *Mengine v. Runyon*, 114 F.3d 415, 418-419 (3d Cir. 1997); *Staub v. Boeing*, 919 F. Supp. 366 (W.D. Wa. 1996).

[23] *Mengine* (3d); Malabarba (7th); *Benson v. Northwest Airlines*, 62 F.3d 1108 (8th Cir.1995); *Barnett v. U.S. Air Inc.*, (9th Cir. 1998).

[24] *Myers v. Hose*, 50 F.3d 278 (4th Cir. 1995); *Vande Zande v. State of Wisconsin Dept. of Administration*, 44 F.3d 538 (7th Cir. 1995).

- Employers are *not* obligated to provide an employee the singular accommodation he or she requests or prefers;[26]

- Employers are *not* required to 'bump' other employees to create a vacancy just to be able to reassign the disabled employee;[27]

- Employers certainly do *not* have to accommodate a disabled employee by promoting him or her to a higher level;[28]

- Employers do *not* have to make an accommodation that would be inconsistent with an existing CBA or contravene the seniority rights of other employees;[29]

- Reasonable accommodation does *not* require employers to eliminate or reassign "essential" job functions;[30]

- Employers do not have to *alter fundamentally* the nature of a job.[31]

Although the federal courts do not appear willing to *require* an employer to transform a temporary light duty accommodation into a permanent position, some have not entirely ruled out the possibility. The Third Circuit has stated that even though an employer is not required to create new jobs or transform its temporary light duty jobs into permanent jobs to accommodate a disability, the court is:

> [R]eluctant to adopt a per se rule that the conversion of a temporary job to a permanent job can never constitute a "reasonable accommodation". . . . We think that in most cases the imposition of such a requirement will be unreasonable, but there might arise the rare case in which the cost of converting the temporary job into a permanent job is slight and the benefits considerable.[32]

---

25 *Carter v. Tisch*, 822 F.2d 465 (4th Cir. 1987) (FRA case citing *dicta* in *Marsh v. Arline*, 480 U.S. 273 (1987)).
26 *Malabarba* (7th).
27 *Id.*
28 *Id.*
29 *Benson v. Northwest Airlines*, 62 F.3d 1108 (8th Cir.1995); *Lujan v. Pacific Maritime Association*, 165 F.3d 738 (9th Cir. 1999); *Willis v. Pacific Maritime Association*, 162 F.3d 561 (9th Cir. 1998).
30 *Barnett* (9th).
31 *Id.*

> Although the federal courts do not appear willing to *require* an employer to transform a temporary light duty accommodation into a permanent position, some have not entirely ruled out the possibility.

There also has been some litigation about how to assess the employer accommodation obligation once an employee has been transferred into a "temporary" light duty position. The primary cases are *Taylor v. Garnett,*[33] a case arising under the Federal Rehabilitation Act, and *Valdez v. Albuquerque Public Schools,*[34] an ADA case.

In both *Taylor* and *Valdez,* the employees had been accommodated by their employers and transferred to light duty, but eventually both were discharged. The main issue in both cases was how to identify which positions the plaintiffs' abilities should be measured against — *their original positions or the "temporary" light duty positions that they occupied at the time of their discharge.* And in both cases (*Valdez* citing *Taylor*), the courts found that the employers had essentially moved the disabled employees into permanent positions and ruled that, for the purposes of the claims, their abilities should be measured against the light duty positions they held when discharged.

Discussion of these two case has focused on the permanent/temporary nature of the disabled employees' light duty jobs. In *Malabarba v. Chicago Tribune Co.,*[35] the plaintiff cited *Taylor* and *Valdez* for the proposition that an employee alleging an ADA violation need only be qualified to perform the essential functions of the light duty position to which he was reassigned in order to meet the "qualified individual with a disability" requirement.

---

[32] *Mengine v. Runyon*, 114 F.3d 415, 418-19 (3d Cir. 1997).
[33] 820 F. Supp. 933 (E.D. Penn., 1993).
[34] 875 F. Supp. 740 (D. N. Mex., 1994).
[35] 149 F.3d 690 (7th Cir. 1998).

The Seventh Circuit, however, distinguished the lower court cases by characterizing them as involving *permanent* light duty reassignments, as opposed to a temporary position. In fact, the *Taylor* court appears to acknowledge the relevance of a permanent/temporary distinction so the Seventh Circuit characterization may be correct.[36] According to the *Taylor* court, it recognized that the employer could legitimately claim that it had placed the employee into temporary light duty with the belief that the employee would only be temporarily injured and that once the disabilities proved permanent, they reserved the right to discharge the employee because the employee could no longer perform the essential functions of his *original* position.

At least one local federal district court, in a case involving the King County Jail, has commented on the *Taylor/Valdez* controversy. In *Kees v. Wallenstein*,[37] fired corrections officers claimed they had been permanently accommodated by the employer. Once again the question was about which position their abilities should be measured against: (1) their *original* position (corrections officer); or (2) their position upon temporary accommodation (reassignment to the control room). The district court ruled against the officers and distinguished *Taylor/Valdez* on the basis that the accommodations made for the corrections officers were temporary, not permanent.[38]

In *Wallenstein*, the employees tried to prove permanency, despite the fact that the employer had a written policy stating that the light duty assignments were temporary. They did this by introducing other evidence showing that the accommodations were permanent (mostly instances of lax enforcement of the policy). The *Kees* court dismissed this evidence by stating that *laxity of policy enforcement would not be enough to rebut the written policy*.[39] The Ninth Circuit later affirmed the District Court.[40]

---

[36] 820 F. Supp. at 938 n.9.

[37] 973 F. Supp. 1191 (1997), *aff'd*, 161 F.3d 1196 (9th Cir. 1998).

[38] 973 F. Supp. at 1196.

[39] *Id.* at 1197.

[40] 161 F.3d 1196 (9th Cir. 1998).

But in *Cripe v City of San Jose,*[41] the Ninth Circuit ruled that the City was obligated to accommodate officers into special duty assignments despite physical injuries that kept the officers from being able to execute forcible arrests. Citing the large size of the department (over 1000 officers), the court expressed doubt that the existence of a limited number of special duty officers unable to respond to an emergency situation was an undue hardship on the City. Taking a position at odds with some other court decisions, the Ninth Circuit panel in *Cripe* concluded that because making a forcible arrest was not required for special duty assignments, an accommodation by assignment to such a position was required.

Because of the differences between the state and federal laws, there has been some uncertainty as to how state courts would approach the subject of permanent light duty jobs for employees, including public safety employees. There is now at least one Court of Appeals decision which rejects an argument that there is a broader state disability discrimination law right for such an accommodation.

Using similar reasoning under state law, a Washington appeals court held in *Dedman v. Personnel Appeals Board,*[42] that there is no obligation of the State Department of Corrections to accommodate a state corrections officer who could not serve in all of the different correction functions in the prison. The court concluded that the "essential function" requirement was *implicit* in the state law as part of a reasonable accommodation test. It rejected the claim that the officer should be accommodated in positions with limited inmate contact, such as control room operator positions.

In *Dedman,* the court also found persuasive the employer's argument it did not have an obligation to restructure the existing position description and that rotating the corrections officers through each various correction officer post served important operational interests. Consequently, it concluded, being able to make inmate contact was an "essential function" which could not be waived.

It remains unclear whether this will be the final resolution of the light duty question in Washington or the Ninth Circuit. The State Supreme Court will likely eventually have to resolve this question, but has not yet addressed this issue squarely.

---

[41] 261 F.3d 877 (9th Cir 2001).

[42] 98 Wn. App. 471, 989 P.2d 1214 (1999).

It remains clear that there is an obligation for employers to accommodate individuals under the state disability law by providing them opportunities to acquire other employment within the employer's workforce. The suggestion arising from the case law is that these employees are entitled to priority consideration before other employees. The courts have yet to clarify how those rights of accommodation will interface with civil service rules.

b. Scheduling Issues

Often, public safety employees have a disability which impairs their ability to work around-the-clock, or, at least, in frequently rotating shifts. As one example of a common disability, diabetes, at least for some individuals, impedes their ability to rotate back and forth through the 24/7 shifts because of the health implications of such schedule changes. There are a variety of other health issues which can be aggravated by shift work.

The federal courts are divided as to whether restructuring the hours of work is a reasonable accommodation.

The federal courts are divided as to whether restructuring the hours of work is a reasonable accommodation. The majority view is that if an accommodation such as this can be made, it should be made. In some departments, though, especially smaller ones, this type of accommodation can have a much greater negative impact on the department's ability to get the work scheduled and, for that reason alone, could be seen as an "undue hardship." In larger departments, this type of accommodation would not normally involve an undue hardship. But it may be an undue hardship within particular classifications where fewer personnel are assigned, and the impacts necessarily are greater.

c. Mental Health Issues

> Where an employee has a mental health problem which impedes their ability to recognize and request assistance, courts have imposed a burden *on the employer* to act unilaterally to begin the interactive process of identifying an accommodation.

Public safety employees, like any other employee, can have mental health issues. Constant stress can aggravate these issues and ultimately affect their ability to perform. In such cases, employees will be entitled to the protection of the disability discrimination laws *to the extent that these issues can be reasonably accommodated.*

Mental illness is certainly a protected disability, but so are other forms of less severe mental health problems, such as post-traumatic stress disorder (PTSD). As with other disabilities, courts have wrestled with the extent of an employer's obligation to accommodate these situations.

Typically an employee seeking an accommodation has the burden to come forth, make the request, and identify the circumstances warranting it. But due to the nature of mental health issues, here the burden is different. The case law has been clear in defining a special accommodation obligation for employers in connection with mental health issues: Where an employee has a mental health problem which impedes their ability to recognize and request assistance, courts have imposed a burden *on the employer* to act unilaterally to begin the interactive process of identifying an accommodation.

d. Physical Fitness Tests

Courts are unlikely to find physical fitness tests to be valid under disability discrimination laws. There have been only a handful of cases addressing this issue yet, but it appears unlikely that these plans will be sustained. Courts have already struck down a number of these plans on gender discrimination grounds. The primary deficiency in these plans is that they do not correlate precisely to the essential functions of the job. *If* they did, they would not be age and gender graded the way they typically are. Since everyone in the job classification must perform the same essential functions, there is no justifiable basis, from the perspective of disability law, to age and gender score such tests.

Some of these plans have premium pay attached for successful test takers. Denial of the premium to an individual with a disability might potentially violate disability discrimination laws. An employer might be able to circumvent this requirement by simply automatically paying the premium amount to any individual who could demonstrate their failure to qualify was directly as a result of their disability.

e. Weight Issues

It is unclear the extent to which disability laws will protect individuals with weight problems. The federal laws do not treat normal overweight as a protected disability.[43] Morbid obesity might qualify as a disability, but federal courts have often looked to whether there is an underlying physiological disability that caused the obesity.[44] Regardless, individuals who are morbidly obese are very unlikely to be able to fulfill the essential functions of most law enforcement and firefighter positions.

The extent to which Washington state disability law may protect overweight individuals is still undefined. Since state law defines disabilities in terms of "abnormalities," it is an open question as to how heavy an individual might be before they are entitled to legal protection.

---

43 *EEOC v. Watkins Motor Lines, Inc.*, 463 F.3d 426 (6th Cir. 2006).
44 *Id.*

f. Alcoholism

There has been some conflict between the ADA, the Rehabilitation Act, and the state disability law concerning whether and how alcoholism can be accommodated. The Rehabilitation Act and the state law do seem to require some degree of accommodation, even when alcoholism produces on-duty job impacts. The ADA, by contrast, has been primarily interpreted *not* to require accommodation of alcoholism to the extent that it involves a violation of a work rule. The divergence in approaches arises from the different language in each statute.

There has been some conflict between the ADA, the Rehabilitation Act, and the state disability law concerning whether and how alcoholism can be accommodated.

Duty to Accommodate. Where the disability at issue involves alcoholism behaviors, the prevailing view of courts under the federal Rehabilitation Act is that the employer has an obligation to provide extensive opportunities for treatment, *even to the point of accommodating short-term relapses which are anticipated to occur.*

While the law does not require the employer to tolerate an *indefinite* number of relapses, it does require the employer to acknowledge that certain relapses might occur and this, in turn, imposes upon the employer the duty to offer additional treatment opportunities.

The seminal case defining an employer's obligation to accommodate alcoholism is a Fourth Circuit decision — *Rodgers v. Lehman*,[45] The Ninth Circuit Court of Appeals has approved and adopted the stringent approach of the Fourth Circuit in its leading decision on this issue — *Fuller v. Frank*.[46] In *Fuller*, the Ninth Circuit defined the reasonable accommodation standards of *Rogers* as requiring "that a governmental employer follow a progression of increasingly severe responses to an employee's alcoholism."[47] Under this *Rodgers/Fuller* standard:

[45] 869 F.2d 243 (4th Cir. 1989).
[46] 916 F.2d 558 (9th Cir. 1990).
[47] *Id.* at 562.

> The employer should 1) inform the employee of available counseling services; 2) provide the employee with a "firm choice" between treatment and discipline; 3) afford an opportunity for outpatient treatment, with discipline for continued drinking or failures to participate; 4) afford an opportunity for inpatient treatment, if outpatient treatment fails; and 5) absent special circumstances, discharge the employee for any further relapse.[48]

While the law does not require the employer to tolerate an *indefinite* number of relapses, it does require the employer to acknowledge that certain relapses might occur and this, in turn, imposes upon the employer the duty to offer additional treatment opportunities.

Although, under federal law, alcoholism is clearly established as a "disability" (with primarily the extent of accommodation at controversy), the Washington State Supreme Court has held that whether alcoholism is a disability is a case-by-case question. In *Phillips v. City of Seattle*,[49] the court held that ultimately whether alcoholism is a qualifying "disability" is a question of fact for the jury to decide. Citing the varied nature of the alcoholic condition and the policy and medical disputes regarding the nature and cause of alcoholism, the court in *Phillips* concluded that the trier of fact should assess in a given case whether the individual alcohol condition constituted a legal disability.

The ADA also provides certain protection for alcoholics in certain circumstances, but more limited than that under state law or under the Federal Rehabilitation Act. The ADA expressly permits employers to "hold an employee who engages in the illegal use of drugs or who is an alcoholic to the same qualification standards for employment or job performance and behavior that such entity holds other employees, even if any unsatisfactory performance or behavior is related to the drug use or alcoholism of such employee."[50] The meaning of this clause has been the source of on-going litigation.

Both the Rehabilitation Act and the ADA prohibit employers from disciplining employees because of their disability. The laws also require affirmative accommodation of alcoholism including multiple treatment opportunities. This much seems to be undisputed.

---

[48] *Id.*
[49] 111 Wn.2d 903, 766 P.2d 1099 (1989).
[50] ADA § 104(C)(4).

The policy of the Rehabilitation Act is aptly stated in *Teahan v. Metro-North Commuter Railroad Co.*:[51]

> This section of the labor law [Section 504 of the Rehabilitation Act] aims to balance the statutory guarantee of equal opportunity for the handicap person so that he or she may become a contributing member of the work force against the rightful concern of an employer that is a recipient of federal funds to preserve the effectiveness of its programs. For an employer to assume that simply because of a handicap an individual is unable to function in a given employment context stereotypes that person, seeing him, as it were, through a glass, darkly. To view a handicapped person in such a simplistic way affects the discrimination forbidden by 504.[52]

At issue in *Teahan* was the termination of an employee who suffered from alcoholism from — which he had since been rehabilitated — after which had an extensive record of absenteeism. The employer had convinced the trial court that by terminating *Teahan* for absenteeism, it was not discriminating against him *because of* his disability, even though it conceded that the absenteeism was caused by the alcoholism. Teahan appealed.

The Second Circuit overturned the district court, holding that the employer's argument would allow *any* employer to "rely" on any conduct as a manifestation or a symptom of a disability, and, in so doing, avoid the burden of proving that the disability is relevant to the job qualifications. The court explained:

> An example may help illustrate this point. An employee has one leg shorter than the other, causing him to limp, which we assume is a "handicap" under Section 504. The limp causes the worker to make a loud "thump" when he takes a step. He is fired, his employer says, because of the thumping. Under the District Court's analysis, the employee may not maintain a suit under Section 504 because the handicap is the limp, not the thump; hence the worker was not fired "solely by reason of" his handicap, but rather because of the attribute caused by the handicap. . . . Yet the proper analysis is that the causal connection between the limp (handicap and the thump, symptomatic manifestation of the handicap) is such that the employer did "rely" on the handicap.[53]

---

[51] 951 F.2d 511 (2d Cir. 1991).
[52] *Id.* at 513.

The Second Circuit's reasoning in *Teahan* has been adopted by a number of other courts. For example, the Sixth Circuit approved this reasoning in another alcohol disability case in *Ferby v. Runyon.*[54]

Teahan was also cited in a controversial district court decision, within the Ninth Circuit, *Ham v. Nevada.*[55] *Ham* involved the ironic termination of Chief of the State of Nevada "Bureau of Alcohol and Drug Abuse" following a drunk driving arrest. The employer argued that they had terminated Ham for the crime of drunk driving, not his alcoholism.

The court rejected this argument and ordered Ham reinstated, reasoning that "since the drunk driving was a causally connected manifestation of the alleged handicap, defendant's actions were admittedly based upon plaintiff's alcoholism." The court added: "Being fired for behavior caused by one's affliction is the same thing as being fired for one's affliction." But other courts have interpreted the ADA and the Rehabilitation Act to allow employers to impose discipline for misconduct *even if directly related to alcoholism.*[56]

The law requires employers to make "reasonable accommodations" of individuals with disabilities, and alcoholism is an established disability under federal law. But the duty to accommodate is not endless. In *Rodgers v. Lehman,*[57] the Fourth Circuit Court of Appeals set forth guidelines for determining when the employer has made a "reasonable accommodation" in connection with an alcoholic employee. Those standards — which have frequently been cited by other courts with approval — involve multiple steps and repeat opportunities:

- When the agency suspects that an employee's poor performance results from alcoholism, it should inform the employee of available counseling services.

---

53 951 F.2d at 515-16.

54 1993 Lexis 20705 (6th Cir. 1993) (unpublished).

55 788 F. Supp. 455 (D. Nev. 1992).

56 *See, e.g., Randall v. Port of Portland*, 8 AD Cases 1404 (1998) (citing *Collings v. Tanguien Fibre Co.*, 73 F.3d 828 (9th Cir. 1993)).

57 869 F.2d 253 (4th Cir. 1989).

- If the employee's unsatisfactory work performance continues, the agency must provide the employee with a "firm choice" between treatment and discipline. The agency must clearly unequivocally warn the employee that unsatisfactory work performance caused by drinking will result in discipline, eventually including the termination of employment.

- Unless in a particular case it is clear that an in-patient treatment is immediately required, the employee must be allowed to participate initially in out-patient treatment of sufficient duration to assure him a reasonable opportunity for cure.

- If the employee continues to drink while participating in that treatment, the agency may impose progressive discipline upon him for any resulting job-related misconduct.

- If the employee ceases to participate in or fails out-patient treatment, discharge is not automatic. Unless the agency can establish that it would suffer an undue hardship from the employee's absence, the agency must, before discharging him, afford him an opportunity to participate in an in-patient program using accrued and unpaid leave.

- If the employee completes the program, but thereafter relapses, and thereafter fails to perform his job satisfactorily, a decision by the agency to discharge him will be *presumed* to be reasonable. Only in the rare case, such as where a recovering alcoholic has had a single relapse after a prolonged period of abstinence, can this presumption be rebutted.[58]

The court explained its reasoning for adopting such an elaborate system:

---

[58] 869 F.2d at 259.

> On the other hand, the nature of the disease of alcoholism requires that there be a continuum of treatment and that the alcoholic be allowed some opportunity for failure in order to come to the acceptance of his disease which is the critical element of his cure. On the other hand, both effective treatment and the needs of the workplace require that an alcoholic employee be firmly confronted with the consequences of his drinking.[59]

In *Fuller v. Frank*,[60] the Ninth Circuit Court of Appeals cited *Rodgers v. Lehman* with approval. The court also adopted as mandatory the multiple accommodation measures defined by the Fourth Circuit in *Lehman*. In *Fuller*, though, the Ninth Circuit concluded, that given the case the employer had more than complied with those steps, including *repeated* treatments and *repeated* leaves of absence, and even ultimately extending a "last chance" agreement. The court stated, "The postal service was not required to provide Fuller with another chance after giving him a 'last chance.' "[61]

ADA and the Workplace Rule Violation. There is a competing set of ADA cases which hold, though, that if the employee engages in a violation of the work rule there is no duty to accommodate the individual. If, for example, a police officer incurs a DUI, he may not be entitled to accommodation, even though a direct result of alcoholism. That probable outcome is a result of the fact that the ADA does not require accommodation of work rule violations, and most police departments have a "work rule" which prohibits violation of criminal laws. Such individuals, though, may have other protection under the Rehabilitation Act and the state disability discrimination law so the ADA would not be pled as a cause of action in a resultant lawsuit.

---

59 *Id.*
60 916 F.2d 558 (9th Cir. 1990).
61 *Id.* at 562.

C. Collective Bargaining and Disability Laws

There are a number of issues that arise concerning the interface of disability laws and the collective bargaining law. The courts have been fairly clear that to the extent an accommodation would *actually violate* the terms of the CBA, the accommodation is *not* reasonable and need not be made. For example, if the CBA contains a shift bidding process, than individual with a disability who seeks an adjustment in the bid process cannot demand that the shift bidding process be altered. But there is also case law that holds that an employer violates the ADA when it fails to at least *ask* a union whether it is willing to enter a memorandum of understanding modifying the CBA.

It is an open question under law what the employer's obligations are when the requested accommodation does not violate an explicit term of the CBA, but is contrary to a "past practice" not expressed in the CBA. There is limited case law on this question, but the prevailing view seems to be that such past practices do not impede the employer's ability to make an accommodation.

This result is reflected in *City of Dearborn Heights*.[62] There the arbitrator faced a claim by the City that it was authorized, as part of its duty to accommodate, to move a police lieutenant who suffered from "brittle diabetes" off of night shift, despite the existence of a past practice of bidding by seniority. The arbitrator concluded that deviation from seniority was a reasonable accommodation under the ADA and should be allowed despite seniority practices. The Arbitrator reasoned that compliance with the collective bargaining agreement was only one factor in assessing whether an accommodation was reasonable, not a controlling factor. He applied a "balancing" of interests approach and concluded the night shift work greatly aggravated a life threatening health condition for the individual officer so that the overall balance favored allowing the out-of-seniority assignment.

It is an open question under law what the employer's obligations are when the requested accommodation does not violate an explicit term of the CBA, but is contrary to a "past practice" not expressed in the CBA.

[62] 101 LA 809 (Kanner 1993.

At the very least, it seems the courts would require that an employer would have to seek out the union's position on whether it was willing to alter an existing past practice. If, after such a modification is requested, and the union indicates it *is willing* to forego prior practices to make an accommodation, it is likely the accommodation is required and that it constitutes unlawful discrimination not to make the accommodation (assuming that it is otherwise reasonable).

Occasionally, employers will seek a broad contractual waiver of the union's bargaining right to allow it to make "whatever changes are required" by the ADA. It is unwise to enter into such a broad waiver because of the unforeseen impact such language may have on the rights of other employees. The better practice is to address the requests for accommodation on a case-by-case basis as they occur, rather than forfeit the union's rights to participation in a discussion about the scope of the allowed accommodations.

Chapter 2: The Right to Privacy: ADA and Other Protections in the Fitness for Duty Examination Process

Public safety employees are in occupations that can take a tremendous physical and mental toll. Public safety employers traditionally have ordered employees to submit to fitness for duty examinations when they suspect that the employees are having difficulty performing the job because of injury, illness, or emotional difficulty. In the past, courts and arbitrators have been deferential to the employers' concern for the welfare of the officers, fellow employees, and the public. The ADA, however, revised many of the past rules.

ADA Guidelines. If an employee can perform the essential functions of the job, the department has no right to request a fitness for duty examination. But if a department has reasonable grounds for believing that an employee cannot perform these essential functions, then it may require the employee to obtain a medical or psychological examination. The examination must be "job related" and "consistent with business necessity."

In the 20 years since the implementation of the ADA, the case law to date remains sparse concerning the justification and evidence needed for an employer to have a sufficient basis to compel a medical or psychological examination. Certainly, if the employee has demonstrable on-the-job problems for which there is no ready explanation, the employer may require a properly focused medical examination to determine if there is a medical cause for the difficulties.

Yin v. California. In its initial case to address this issue, the Ninth Circuit court indicated some degree of deference to management's claims of business necessity. In *Yin v. California*,[63] the court ruled that an employee's claim — that she had been improperly compelled to submit to a medical examination when there was no demonstrated inability to perform the job — lacked merit. The individual had an attendance record that involved an advanced amount of sick leave usage. There had also been some indications of on-the-job impacts from these illnesses. Under these circumstances, the court reasoned that there was a sufficient business necessity to compel an examination.

---

[63] 95 F.3d 864 (9th Cir. 1996).

Brownfield v. City of Yakima. More recently, in *Brownfield v. City of Yakima,*[64] the Ninth Circuit explained that the business necessity test is not limited to situations where the employee has demonstrated an inability to do the job. The court ruled that business necessity might also apply to "prophylactic" examinations to determine fitness, "especially when the employer is engaged in dangerous work."

In *Brownfield,* an officer periodically would become enraged during interactions with management. After several incidents, one of which involved the officer becoming "consumed" with anger and fear about his community service partner, the department referred him for a fitness exam. A psychologist concluded that the officer was unfit for duty. A later examination by his doctor cleared him for duty, after which the department wanted an additional examination. He refused the additional examination and was terminated for insubordination. The Ninth Circuit then addressed the legality of the fitness examination order.

The court explained the employer's right to request an examination was real but not limitless

---

The City of Yakima argued that it had a business necessity.[65] The Ninth Circuit agreed, concluding that the department did not violate the ADA because it had a reasonable and legitimate reason to doubt the officer's ability to perform the duties of a police officer.

The court explained that the employer's right to request an examination was real, but not limitless:

> In interpreting the "business necessity" standard in another ADA context, we have cautioned that it "is quite high, and is not to be confused with mere expediency."

The court explained that an "employee's behavior cannot be merely annoying or inefficient to justify an examination; rather, there must be genuine reason to doubt whether that employee can perform job-related functions."

---

[64] 612 F.3d 1140 (9th Cir. Wash. 2010).

[65] *Brownfield,* 612 F.3d 1140.

The court further explained in *Brownfield* that the justification test must be an "objective" one, applying the "reasonable person" standard. It also held, despite granting employers the right to do "prophylactic" examinations, that the burden of demonstrating "business necessity" fell upon the employer. It explained that especially in the context of law enforcement work, some deference would be extended to the employer's judgment:

> Brownfield attempts to explain away each incident by providing background facts suggesting his reactions were entirely reasonable and by challenging the third-party reports as factually inaccurate, but he does not dispute that he reacted as described or that the third-party reports were made to the YPD. Although a minor argument with a coworker or isolated instances of lost temper would likely fall short of establishing business necessity, Brownfield's repeated volatile responses are of a different character. Moreover, our consideration of the FFDEs' [Fitness for Duty Examination] legitimacy is heavily colored by the nature of Brownfield's employment. Police officers are likely to encounter extremely stressful and dangerous situations during the course of their work. *See Watson*, 177 F.3d at 935 ("Police departments place armed officers in positions where they can do tremendous harm if they act irrationally."). When a police department has good reason to doubt an officer's ability to respond to these situations in an appropriate manner, an FFDE is consistent with the ADA. Reasonable cause to question Brownfield's ability to serve as a police officer was present here.[66]

Causes triggering a fit for duty examination. There are a number of circumstances under which the employer might have a right to compel a medical examination:

- The employee indicates a disability and requests an accommodation;
- It appears that the employee might have a medical limitation that could interfere with the job;
- There is an unexplained performance deficiency;
- The employer has complied with the EEOC requirements to establish a "periodic physical examination" of the employees — the program must

[66] *Id.* at 1146-47.

be as established under "federal, state or local law" and be consistent with the ADA.

Scope of Report. The ADA was drafted with a lack of clarity regarding the role of the doctor and what the doctor can report to the employer. Courts have yet to clarify what those restrictions are, but at least one plausible reading of the statute is that the doctor is only permitted to report to the employer the information narrowly focused on whether the employee can perform the specific job and what accommodations might be needed to assist in performing the job. Although it is a common practice for doctors to release the entire medical report, it appears that this practice might be illegal under the ADA.

Often, the employer or the doctor will try to get the employee to sign a "waiver" that would allow the doctor to make unrestricted reports to the employer. The legality of these waivers is doubtful.

Often, the employer or the doctor will try to get the employee to sign a "waiver" that would allow the doctor to make unrestricted reports to the employer. The legality of these waivers is doubtful. Although the employee is obligated to cooperate with valid medical examinations, there is no legal basis for either the employer or the doctor to require employees to waive whatever legal rights they may have under the ADA if the reports are made in contravention of the statute. Employees or union representatives who are presented with the issue of a required waiver form should seek legal counsel concerning their response to the request.

Confidentiality of medical information. The ADA contains strict requirements for maintaining the confidentiality of the medical information once it is disseminated to the employer. Medical reports are to be maintained in separate medical files, and access is restricted to designated individuals. The ADA requires that supervisors and managers may be informed about specific work limitations, but not about the nature of the medical condition.

The ADA does not define who is a "manager." Is the police chief a "manager?" If so, only the doctor the employer contracts with has the right to hold the information. Or is there someone at the top of the employer's management pyramid who has a right to this information? The courts have yet to decide these issues.

Sick leave verification. Another common practice for employers — which is likely in violation of the ADA — is to record specific medical information on sick leave request or verification forms. First, unless there is a history of sick leave abuse, it is unlikely that the employer is entitled to *any* information concerning the reason the employee is sick on a given day. Second, even if there is a business necessity for requiring this information, it *must* be maintained as a separate medical report and cannot be retained in a general personnel file or file of leave records.

Chapter 3: The Right to Job Security: Protections of the CBA and the Application of Just Cause

Law enforcement and firefighters in the state are typically covered by a "dual" appeal system — civil service and a labor contract that usually contains a "just cause" requirement. The way these systems operate and the elements of "just cause" are beyond the intended scope of this book. But in this brief chapter we did want to alert you to the ways in which the just cause requirements protect your employees when they are facing termination due to injury or other disability.

A wrongfully discharged employee has the right to bring a lawsuit in court, asserting the disability rights discussed in Chapter 1. But the CBA also may offer some degree of protection. So we will discuss the "just cause" standards as they apply in arbitration in this situation. We are assuming for purposes of this Chapter that a separated employee who wanted to appeal would do so under the labor contract, not civil service. The difference in the two systems is beyond the scope of this booklet, but suffice it to say that we would rarely recommend selecting the civil service forum where arbitration was available.

The "just cause" standard which includes a variety of "tests" applies more clearly to discipline-related discharges. Assuming that your labor contract includes all "discharges" within the just cause requirement, the employer would also have the burden to prove that a medical related separation was also for cause. The tests to apply and the nature of the burden are not the same as in a discipline case, though.

Arbitrators generally recognize that principles of just cause incorporate statutes prohibiting discrimination.[67] This is especially the case where a collective bargaining agreement contains a non-discrimination clause.[68] This approach extends as well to the law regarding disabilities.[69]

---

[67] Elkouri & Elkouri, *supra*, at 85 (4th Ed. 1985-87 Supplement).

[68] *Id.*

[69] Bornstein & Gosline, *supra*, at § 21.11; *see, also, Goodman v. Employment Security Dept.*, 69 Wn. App. 98 (1993) (Personnel Appeals Board should consider alleged breaches of collective bargaining agreements).

A. Misconduct Related to Disabilities.

Addiction-related behaviors, even where arbitrators did not apply the standard under disability discrimination statutes, have been recognized to be mitigating factors justifying reinstatement. In *Ohio State Highway Patrol,*[70] the arbitrator reinstated a state trooper who was convicted of a drunk driving charge where the trooper was making successful progress in an alcohol treatment program. While the arbitrator acknowledged that law enforcement personnel are held to a higher standard, she concluded that the employer had failed to give the employee's effort at rehabilitation the weight it deserved as "distinctive and crucial mitigating factors."[71] In *Phillips 66 Company,*[72] the arbitrator held that the grievant's gambling addiction which resulted in excessive absenteeism, constituted a mitigating factor warranting reinstatement.

Addiction-related behaviors, even where arbitrators did not apply the standard under disability discrimination statutes, have been recognized to be mitigating factors justifying reinstatement.

The question of how far employers must go to accommodate disabilities, including addictions such as alcoholism, was discussed in greater extent in Chapter 1. The main point to bear in mind is that those Chapter 1 principles can apply if an employee is being separated for reasons that might violate state or federal disability discrimination laws.

These laws offer employees extensive protection *if they are diagnosed alcoholics and seeking treatment.* Arbitrators usually find the "just cause" standard incorporates these legal requirements. Employees who are not alcoholics often have less protection for alcohol-related misconduct. And even employees who are alcoholics are not insulated from behavior that violates work rules. Though courts and arbitrators are divided on this point, most have held that disability discrimination laws do not require an accommodation that permits the violation of a reasonable work rule.

---

[70] 96 L.A. 613 (Bittel, 1991).

[71] 96 L.A. at 619; *see also, Ashland Petroleum Co.*, 90 L.A. 681 (Volz, 1988) (reinstating employee who participated in rehabilitation program for drug use after the discharge; arbitrator noting that addictive behaviors involve denials which are often only overcome in "crisis situation").

[72] 88 L.A. 617 (Weisbrod, 1987).

Disability discrimination laws offer little or no protection for employees who are current substance abusers of illegal narcotics. Therefore, those employees are not entitled to any accommodation, especially when they work in a law enforcement department.

Arbitrators will generally find these disability laws implied into the just cause standard. Often contracts also explicitly incorporate these provisions through an anti-discrimination clause. Even prior to the enactment of disability discrimination laws, the majority view of arbitrators which has developed is that alcoholics who are in recovery and treatment are entitled to some opportunity to demonstrate rehabilitation.

Where an employee engages in conduct that is alcohol-related, yet is not a diagnosed alcoholic, separate and apart from the "just cause" requirements, *such an employee has no particular protection under disability laws.* Experience indicates that this dichotomy under the law for those who declare their status as alcoholics and those that deny they are alcoholics — once clearly explained to employees caught in the cross-hairs of an alcohol-related misconduct investigation — is the most forceful inducement known to trigger a trip to rehabilitation, often overcoming years of denial.

Some employers have rules prohibiting off-duty public intoxication. It is questionable whether most arbitrators would find such rules to be reasonable or lawful, except to the extent there is a demonstrable impact on fitness for duty. But employees who engage in criminal conduct or other conduct rising to the level of "conduct unbecoming an officer" while intoxicated, as discussed above, may face serious discipline.

Separate from nondiscrimination statutes, most arbitrators have interpreted the just cause standard as an *independent source* of legal protection for recovering alcoholics. Even before disability discrimination laws were enacted, arbitrators had developed guidelines addressing the extent of accommodation required for the recovering alcoholic employee. There is no single consensus position on this controversial subject. One observer identified three distinct arbitral approaches to alcoholism:

1. Hold all employees to the same standards of conduct, without regard to the nature or severity of their substance abuse problems or their efforts to seek assistance.

2. Give special consideration to employees who have acknowledged to the employer that they have a substance abuse problem, and who actively seek help in resolving the problem before discharge.

3. Treat substance abuse as a "disease," and accommodate it like other diseases.[73]

The first hard line approach is a distinctly minority view. Most arbitrators approach alcohol problems with some blend of the second and third approaches. And this tendency to give treatment opportunities has accelerated in light of disability laws.

In *Phillip Morris*,[74] Arbitrator Volz set out five common sense principles that should be considered in handling alcoholism in the context of discipline. These provide a good framework for understanding how most arbitrators will treat this issue:

- First, progressive discipline is ineffective in improving employee reliability until the employee recognizes that he is an alcoholic.

- Second, an alcoholic will usually not recognize the disease until faced with a crisis such as termination.

- Third, post-discharge evidence is relevant and admissible in alcohol-related arbitrations to show the extent of the alcoholic's rehabilitation.

- Fourth, in assessing rehabilitation, the arbitrator should consider more than the alcoholic's word.

- Fifth, a return to employment is often part of the treatment, during which time the employer can determine the employee's progress through monitoring, attitude and adjustment to work.

---

[73] Bornstein & Gosline, *supra*, at § 18.10.
[74] 99 LA 1017 (Volz, 1992).

As indicated, Chapter 1 contains an extensive discussion about how alcoholism is accommodated under disability discrimination laws. Because arbitrators generally find these legal standards implied into CBAs, the principles laid out in that discussion should be understood to integrate with the five principles described above by Arbitrator Volz.

B. Arbitrations Concerning Fitness for Duty Separation.

Employees with physical or mental conditions that interfere with their ability to perform the job functions are potentially protected under state and federal disability discrimination laws. The rights of employees under given circumstances is discussed in greater detail later in a chapter addressing the legal rights of injured and disabled employees.

Employees with physical or mental conditions that interfere with their ability to perform the job functions are potentially protected under state and federal disability discrimination laws.

Arbitrators generally hold that the "just cause" requirement implicitly incorporates the mandates of state and federal disability discrimination laws. Therefore, they will require employers to comply with any legal duty they may have to accommodate an employee.

General standard. Nonetheless, there sometimes comes a time where it is clear that the employee is not capable of performing the job because of physical or mental limitations. Arbitrators have held that where it is established that the employee cannot and will not be able to perform the job, this is in itself just cause for discharge.

The challenging situations arise where the employee is recovering, but the progress of recovery is uncertain. Employers will sometimes object to being compelled to maintain an opening for an employee. Arbitrators have approached this problem from a rule of reason: The employer will be required to maintain the employee on a leave status (unpaid, if paid leaves have been exhausted) *if there is a reasonable prospect that the employee can return in a reasonable amount of time.* But when either the prospects of recovery are low or in the distant future, an arbitrator will generally hold that the employer is justified in discharging the employee.[75]

One expedient way to address this challenge is through contract negotiations by adopting a provision of the civil service rules allowing for "medical reinstatement." Some jurisdictions have created civil service rights, placing medically disabled individuals on a medical reinstatement register, giving these individuals priority for reinstatement, up to a period of time, if there is a recovery.

Mental health. Arbitrators have occasionally had to address the issue of employees whose mental health difficulties create a potential hazard in the workplace. Employers are under an obligation to reasonably accommodate an employee with a disability, but not if such accommodation would create a safety hazard.[76] Before an employer can discharge or discipline an employee with mental health problems, it must conduct some type of investigation into the reasons for the employee's conduct.[77] As one leading arbitration treatise indicates:

> Most arbitrators have been less willing to uphold disciplinary action for violation of shop rules where the employee's conduct was caused by mental health problems that were treatable or in a state of remission, or where the employee had apparently recovered as a result of subsequent treatment.[78]

---

[75] *Compare Fleet Combat Training Center, Pac. Agency*, 82-1 ARB ¶8099, 3482 (Ross, 1981) (holding employer required to accommodate employee who missed a third of work and needed to restructure hours when recovery uncertain, even though employee's missed work seriously burdened the employer) *with Packaging Corp. of Am.,* 105 LA 591 (Hewitt, 1995) (termination of combat-veteran employee with stress reaction upheld despite fact that employee was receiving treatment, but had not yet recovered).

[76] *Johnson Am. Corp.*, 114 LA 577 (D'Eletto, 2000).

[77] Bornstein & Gosline, *supra*, at § 23.09.

[78] *Id.*

The treatise further indicates that:

> There is a general consensus that when medical evidence indicates that a worker's mental disability exposes that employee or others to serious risk of injury or harm, or, alternatively prevents that employee from performing his or her duties, dismissal may be justified.[79]

It then adds:

> In determining whether an employee represents a direct threat to the health or safety of the employee or others, the following factors should be considered:
>
> - The duration of the risk;
> - The nature and severity of the potential harm;
> - The likelihood that the potential harm will occur; and
> - The imminence of the potential harm.

"Direct threat" to safety. The determination of direct threat must rely on objective factual evidence and not on subjective perceptions, irrational fears, patronizing attitudes or stereotypes. Likewise, whether the employee poses a safety risk must be based on an individual evaluation, and not on generalizations about their medical conditions.[80] The determination must be based on the circumstances of the individual under consideration, and the evidence must be compelling and supported by expert opinion.[81] It is impermissible for an employer to simply *assume* that a mental or physical condition automatically makes an employee unfit for work.

---

[79] *Id.*
[80] *See* Elkouri & Elkouri, *supra*, n. 31.
[81] *Id.* (emphasis supplied).

Like the balancing test required when determining whether employers must accommodate disabilities, the ADA requires that employers conduct a similar balancing test when determining whether a disabled employee presents a significant safety hazard to warrant termination.[82] Therefore, employers are required to accommodate disabilities, but they need not create or prolong a safety hazard for their employees, including the one with the mental or physical condition. The employer must balance the interest of the disabled employee in continued employment with the interests of all parties that could potentially be affected by the safety risk posed by that disability, including the affected employee.

In an illustrative case, an employee was terminated because he had homicidal intentions towards many of his coworkers, which came to light during a review of his medical records.[83] The union argued that as the threats were not directed at anyone in particular, there was no real threat. But the arbitrator sided with the employer, stating that the employee appeared to be a "ticking time-bomb" and creates an undue risk to the district, as well as other employees.[84] In considering the balancing of interests, the arbitrator, concluded "[t]he consequences are too grave and the probability of such death threats being carried out is simply too high."

In another case, the employee had been fit for duty with medication, but when he went off his medication, he threatened and endangered co-workers.[85] The arbitrator agreed that the employee would work safely on the medication. But because he had already caused a hazard, the damage had been done, and the arbitrator concluded that an impermissible hazard existed that the employer no longer had to accommodate.[86]

Medical conditions. Many medical restrictions do not qualify as "disabilities" under the ADA, and, therefore, do not require accommodations by the employer. As we will discuss later, Washington law is somewhat more protective of employees with medical disabilities. The extent to which an arbitrator finds just cause to exist or to be lacking will often turn on their interpretation of these statutes.

---

[82] Elkouri & Elkouri, *supra*, n. 31.
[83] *Anchorage School Dist.*, 119 LA 1313 (DiFalco, 2004).
[84] *Id.* at 1320.
[85] *Anchor Hocking*, 125 LA 312 (Cohen, 2008).
[86] *Id.*

In one case, an employee had a medical restriction that did not allow him to work more than 9.5 hours a week.[87] The employer eventually reassigned the employee to a lesser paid former position with shorter shifts. The employee grieved, requesting an accommodation. The arbitrator sided with the employer. Because the hour restriction would not qualify under the ADA as substantially limiting major life activities, the restriction does not have to be accommodated.[88] Following the expansion of the definition of "disability" under the ADAAA,[89] employers will have to accommodate a wider range of disabilities than before.[90] And a different result could occur in Washington's more expansive definition of "disability."

> The degree of proof required by arbitrators in unfitness cases is conflicted and controversial.

Proving unfitness. Unless the employee admits to being unfit for duty, the burden of proof rests on the employer to establish the actual lack of fitness, though there are questions as to the extent of this burden. At a minimum, this burden typically requires a fitness for duty exam by an appropriate health professional. During this process, the employee or the union are allowed to obtain and present a second opinion. In the event there is a dispute, but the employer insists on proceeding to termination, it will ultimately be up to an arbitrator to make the determination.

The degree of proof required by arbitrators in unfitness cases is conflicted and controversial. Many arbitrators defer to management's determination on such issues and relax the burden of proof below what it would be under the traditional "just cause" standard. The majority approach on fitness discharge cases is to assess them under a deferential "arbitrary and capricious" standard. The arbitration cases applying this standard often focus on whether the employer had a "good faith" belief that medical evidence supported the employer action without regard to whether sufficient proof existed in fact. Especially in light of these cases, it is important for the union to present any competing medical opinions before the discharge decision is made.

---

[87] *DelMonte Foods*, 121 LA 1100 (Miles, 2005).

[88] *Id. See also City of Minneapolis*, 125 LA 558 (Befort, 2008) (holding employee with 50lb lifting restriction does not have disability under ADA as lifting restrictions of no more than 25lbs have been recognized).

[89] 42 U.S.C. § 12102

[90] *See generally Paige v. Jefferson Transit Authority*, 2009 WL 2057045 (W.D.Wash. 2011), for a discussion of the expansion of the ADA under the ADAAA.

It is a best practice to negotiate for CBA language that clearly states that both discipline and "discharges" are subject to just cause.

Some CBAs require medical arbitration proceedings in which the two health professionals agree on a third professional. This approach is not advisable, though. There may be a number of legal arguments the union may be able to bring which the medical professional would be inclined to overlook and not be in a meaningful position to assess. For example, often the issue concerning fitness for duty turns on whether an accommodation is reasonable, and arbitrators are better qualified to judge the "reasonableness" of such an accommodation than is a medical professional.

It is a best practice to negotiate for CBA language that clearly states that both discipline and "discharges" are subject to just cause. Absent such language, arbitrators will be more inclined to relieve employers of some of their burden of proof and apply a deferential "good faith" standard for determining whether the discharge was valid. Such a deferential standard weakens your tenure protection and could even bypass the important question of whether the medical evidence even establishes any actual unfitness.

Leave Exhaustion. The question surrounding the exhaustion or nonexhaustion of FMLA leave (discussed in the next chapter) and contractual leaves (sick leave, annual leave, and other paid leaves) appears as a frequent source of confusion concerning separation from employment. The confusion reigns often on both sides.

Some employers believe that once the FMLA or contract leave is exhausted, just cause for separation exists. But that is not the law. Disability laws may require leave as an accommodation and the extent of that leave may exceed the time allowed under either the FMLA or under remaining contract leave balances. There is no inherent conflict here. What employers need to understand is that *even when* these leave balances are exhausted, employees may have a right, dependent upon the circumstances, to continue on *unpaid* leave.

On the other hand, unions or their members also frequently misunderstand the obligation of an employer to continue on payroll a clearly disqualified an employee. The often asserted claim by unions or their members is that the employer must allow the employee to discharge all paid leaves before termination. But that is not the law. If an employee has no reasonable prospect of ever returning, an employer may have just cause to terminate *even if* paid leave time remains on the books. The employer is obligated to afford the employee due process to ascertain that there is not a reasonable prospect for return, but once that duty has been discharged, the employer is allowed to terminate and the existing leave banks would be liquidated according to the terms of the CBA.

Chapter 4: The Right to Leave: The Protections of the FMLA for Self and Others

The Family Medical Leave Act (FMLA)[91] offers additional protection to pregnant employees, and to other individuals who are injured or disabled. In fact, it protects nearly all individuals who may, at some point during their careers, have some family crisis requiring their absence from the workplace.

The FMLA does not mandate that the leave be paid. But where the employee has paid leave available, the employer *must* allow the employee to draw on those leave banks.

The Federal Family Medical Leave Act is designed to balance the interests of employees and their families alongside the interests of the employer to maintain a productive work force. The FMLA essentially supersedes the earlier enacted state family leave law, in that its terms are more generous than had existed in the state law. The state law, though, remains on the books in the event the federal law is ever repealed or modified.

Under the FMLA, an employee is entitled to up to 12 work weeks of family leave in any 12-month period for family leave purposes. Family leave purposes include care of a newborn child, a newly adopted child, or care of a family member — child, spouse or parent — with a "serious health condition." The FMLA also permits leave for the employee's own "serious health condition."[92]

The FMLA does not mandate that the leave be paid. But where the employee has paid leave available, the employer *must* allow the employee to draw on those leave banks.[93] And once those leave banks are exhausted, the FMLA requires employers to allow employees to go out on unpaid leave status for the balance of the permitted time.

---

[91] 29 U.S.C. § 2601.
[92] 29 U.S.C. § 2612(a)(1).
[93] 29 C.F.R. § 825.207(a) (2014).

At the end of the FMLA leave, employees have the right to return to the same position or "an equivalent position with equivalent pay, benefits and working conditions."

Although, as indicated, the FMLA does not require that employees (apart from their access to existing leave banks) be paid their wages, it does mandate the continuation of one important form of compensation. It requires that the employer continue existing health benefits and maintain its payment of its designated share of the premium for those benefits.[94]

At the end of the FMLA leave, employees have the right to return to the same position or "an equivalent position with equivalent pay, benefits and working conditions."[95] An employee's leave may not involve a forfeiture of accrued benefits or seniority that an employee has had prior to taking a leave, but it does not require employers to continue accrual of such seniority-based privileges while out on leave (unless the employer allows such privileges for other forms of leave).[96] In other words, the employee's seniority time will be "tolled" during the leave of absence, but seniority may not be forfeited.

To establish that the leave is *bona fide*, the employer has the right to obtain and seek a "certification" from a health care provider to substantiate the need for the leave. This requirement applies whether the requested leave is for the employee or the employee's family member.[97]

Under the ADA, if the employer has a bona fide reason to question the employee's fitness, it can demand a fitness for duty examination. But under the FMLA it cannot delay returning the employee to pay status *once the employee presents a medical return to work certification.*

[94] 29 U.S.C. § 2614(c).
[95] 29 U.S.C. § 2614(a).
[96] 29 C.F.R. § 825.215(c) (2014).
[97] 29 U.S.C. § 2613.

According to the FMLA, the employer may also demand a "certification of fitness" upon the employee's return.[98] But often there is confusion as to the distinction between this certification and a fitness certification. There is no confusion in the law itself, but often the employer or the employees incorrectly confuse or even conflate the two separate requirements.

In public safety work, injured employees reentering occurs all the time. An employee is injured, later recovers, indicates an ability to return and the employer, upon learning of this, is unsure whether the employee is fit or not. Under the ADA, if the employer has a bona fide reason to question the employee's fitness, it can demand a fitness for duty examination. But under the FMLA it cannot delay returning the employee to pay status *once the employee presents a medical return to work certification.*

This point is well demonstrated in the 2013 decision from the State Supreme Court in *Chaney v. Providence Health Care.*[99] Chaney developed health issues, and the hospital directed him submit to a fitness exam from their selected doctor. He agreed, but first went to his own physician. The two physicians provided competing explanations as to his fitness for duty. Later he was released by his doctor to return. The employer declined to accept his doctor's certification, arguing that it was ambiguous. It then fired him when his allowed leave expired.

The Court ruled that Providence Hospital erred by not accepting Chaney return to work certification even though it thought it was ambiguous:

> When an employee is placed on leave, the FMLA permits employers to require a note from the employee's doctor stating that the employee is fit to work before reinstating the employee. The note need be only a simple statement that the employee is able to return to work. The only other requirement is that the statement must be made at the same time the employee is able to return to work. *Under the FMLA, if these requirements are met, an employer must reinstate the employee. If the employer is concerned about the adequacy of the fitness for work statement, it may seek a clarification from the employee's health care provider but may not delay returning the employee to work.*[100]

---

[98] 29 C.F.R. § 825.312 (2014).
[99] 176 Wn.2d 757, 295 P.2d 728 (2013).
[100] 176 Wn.2d at 738.

The employer is not without recourse if it genuinely believes the employee may not be fit. The Supreme Court is not saying an unfit employee must be returned to duty. The employee must be returned to *pay status*. The employee does not have to linger on paid or unpaid leave that might not have even been requested in the first place. Once the employee seeks to return to work and has a certification to support the request, the employer cannot delay that return to debate the merits of the certification.

The FMLA benefit does not cover most part-time employees. To be eligible, an employee must have worked at least 1250 hours in the prior 12 month period.[101] FMLA allows exemptions of certain "key employees." Key employees are those included in the highest "10%" of pay on the employer's payroll.[102] This requirement could conceivably impact the FMLA coverage of certain mid-level managers in a given public safety department.

A common pitfall for employers relates to the duration of the leave. The law permits the employer to count paid leave used while an individual is medically unable to work toward the 12-week FMLA period. But in order to do so, the employer must give *notice* to the employee that their 12 weeks have begun to run, although such notice may be retroactive "provided that the employer's failure to timely designate leave does not cause harm or injury to the employee."[103]

When an employer, for example, allows an employee to use all their paid sick leave and vacation leave without providing the FMLA notice period, a 12-week period of unpaid leave will then commence *following* the exhaustion of the paid leave. Understandably, this has caused some headaches for personnel directors who have difficulty determining when an individual has begun a long-term period of absence from the workplace. For this reason, employees are often placed on FMLA leave status even though they did not specifically invoke the FMLA. The employer is simply trying to "start the clock" for their own benefit.

When the need for the leave is "foreseeable," the statute requires that employees provide advance notice of not less than 30 days.[104] A good example of a "foreseeable" need for leave is in the case of pregnancy-related leave.

---

[101] 29 C.F.R. § 825.110 (2014).
[102] 29 U.S.C. § 2614.
[103] 29 C.F.R. § 825.301(d) (2014).
[104] 29 U.S.C. § 2612 (e)(1).

Another complication under this statute is addressing medical situations where an employee can work some, but not every day. The FMLA requires the accommodation of these employees, allowing them to take intermittent days off.[105] The statute regulates how employees will get the notice and manage the taking of such intermittent time. These rules grant management a right to transfer such employees into alternative positions with equivalent pay and benefits, if such a transfer would prove less disruptive to the workforce.

The FMLA is essentially an amendment and a separate statute under the Fair Labor Standards Act. As a result, all available FLSA remedies are also generally available under the FMLA.

The FMLA provides an *additional* protection for employees. *It is not designed to remove or limit whatever protections employees otherwise have under the ADA or the CBA.*

This issue is likely to arise in the context of a continued request for an accommodation of an individual who has a physical limitation and whose condition continues after the expiration of the FMLA period. Some employers are under the misimpression that once the FMLA period expires, they have automatic grounds to discharge an employee. This may be true under some circumstances, but it is certainly not always true.

The FMLA and disability law requirements are separate and distinct. And under the CBA just cause requirement, employers have an ongoing obligation to retain an individual on the payroll *as long as there is a reasonable prospect for the return in a reasonable amount of time.* The FMLA does not alter this "just cause" mandate.

As discussed above, state and federal disability laws may require a leave of absence as a medical accommodation in some circumstances *and mere expiration of the FMLA 12 week period does not alter that mandate.* And most arbitrators would find these disability law mandates also to be an implied requirement of the CBA.

---

[105] 29 U.S.C. § 2612 (b)(1).

In short, an employee may have exhausted their statutory FMLA period (and the accompanying paid health insurance benefit), but that does not bar them from requesting continued leave (paid or unpaid) as a medical accommodation. Just as with the FLSA wage and overtime requirements, the FMLA establishes a floor, not a ceiling.

Chapter 5: The Right to Protection from Pregnancy Discrimination: The PDA and Other Related Laws

A. The ADA and Pregnancy

Pregnant employees have significant protection under the Pregnancy Discrimination Act (PDA) and the Family Medical Leave Act (FMLA). This section considers those rights below. The condition of pregnancy is accorded fewer protections under the ADA than the other statutes.

One major hurdle preventing pregnant employees from invoking the ADA is that *pregnancy is not considered a disability.* Although the ADA does not expressly exclude pregnancy from coverage, the implementing regulations do. The EEOC, in its adoption of the interpretative regulations implementing the ADA, stated that pregnancy is *not* a disability and, as a direct result, is not covered by the ADA.[106] The federal courts have concurred, primarily because they have looked to the EEOC's interpretations for guidance.[107]

But pregnant employees invoke ADA if they develop pregnancy-related medical complications, assuming that that these complications would themselves be considered disabilities under the ADA. Back pain or high blood pressure are examples of pregnancy-related conditions that *may* be covered under the ADA. Both the EEOC[108] and the federal courts[109] specifically agree with this conclusion.

---

[106] *Appendix to Part 1630 — Interpretive Guidance on Title I of the Americans with Disabilities Act*, ADA Manual, 70:0109. ("It is important to distinguish between conditions that are impairments and physical, psychological, environmental, cultural and economic characteristics that are not impairments. . . . . Other conditions, such as pregnancy, that are not the result of a physiological disorder are also not impairments.")

[107] *Byerly v. Herr Foods, Inc.*, 2 A.D. Cas. (BNA) 666, 669 (E.D. Pa 1993) (Holding ADA "clearly indicates that pregnancy was not to be considered an impairment covered by the Act."); *Gabriel v. City of Chicago*, 9AD Cas. (BNA) 483, 488 (N.D. Ill. 1998) (holding pregnancy, absent abnormal or unusual circumstances, is not a disability).

[108] *EEOC: Definition of the Term 'Disabilty'*, ADA Manual, 70:1137.

[109] *Cerrato v. Durham*, 5 A.D. Cas. (BNA) 1660 (S.D.N.Y 1996) (applying analysis that distinguishes between normal, uncomplicated pregnancy and complications arising out of pregnancy that, under certain circumstances, can constitute "disability" under ADA); *Patterson v. Xerox Corp.*, 4 Cas. (BNA) 1602 (N.D. Ill. 1995) (holding contention that pregnancy-related severe back pain qualified as disability under the ADA sufficient to withstand motion to dismiss).

On the other hand, the mere presence of an impairment, however, does not automatically mean that an employee has a "disability" as defined under the ADA. This question, instead, will turn on whether the impairment substantially limits, or is regarded as substantially limiting, a major life activity.[110] For these reasons, a pregnant employee seeking protection of disability law would be far more likely to invoke the more liberal protections of the WLAD.

B. Elements of the PDA

Under the Pregnancy Discrimination Act (PDA),[111] employers are prohibited from discriminating against employees because of or on the basis of pregnancy, childbirth, or related medical conditions. The PDA also requires that pregnant employees be treated the same for *all* employment-related purposes, including receipt of benefits under fringe benefit programs, as other persons not so affected *but similar in their ability or inability to work.*

To establish a "prima facie" case of discrimination under Title VII, a plaintiff may prove her claim either through direct evidence, statistical proof, or the test established by the Supreme Court in *McDonnell Douglas Corp. v Green.*[112] Pregnant employees have been most successful under the PDA when they can show that the employer took an adverse employment action *specifically because* of their pregnancy *or* when they can use the *McDonnell Douglas* test to demonstrate an inconsistency in the employer's actions.[113]

[110] ADA Manual, 70:1138.

[111] 42 U.S.C. § 2000e(k).

[112] 411 U.S. 792 (1973). The test requires that the plaintiff show: (1) she was a member of a protected class; (2) she was qualified for the position she lost; (3) she suffered an adverse employment action; and (4) that others similarly situated were more favorably treated. The employer then has an opportunity to offer a non-discriminatory reason for its action. Finally, if the employer offers a reason, the employee has an opportunity to show that the offered reason was a pretext.

[113] *See Adams v. Nolan*, 962 F.2d 791 (1992) (upholding finding in favor of pregnant police officer denied light duty job on grounds pregnancy is non-occupational injury when male officer with non-occupational injury was later given job).

C. The Interplay of the ADA and the PDA

Individually, the ADA and the PDA do not specifically grant pregnant employees the right to on-the-job accommodations. However, when the two acts work in conjunction with each other, they may give pregnant employees extensive protection. The ADA requires employers to accommodate their qualified disabled workers and the PDA requires that pregnant employees be treated the same as those employees similarly situated in their ability or inability to work. Therefore, the PDA allows pregnant employees to tag along with many employees covered by the ADA.

The U.S. Supreme Court held that if an employer "accommodates most nonpregnant employees with lifting limitations while categorically failing to accommodate pregnant employees with lifting limitations," the employer may have violated the PDA.[114]

This does not mean that *any* accommodation in *any circumstance* means that an employer must accommodate pregnant employees – the Court rejected the argument that:

> [a]s long as an employer provides one or two workers with an accommodation—say, those with particularly hazardous jobs, or those whose workplace presence is particularly needed, or those who have worked at the company for many years, or those who are over the age of 55—then it must provide similar accommodations to *all* pregnant workers (with comparable physical limitations), irrespective of the nature of their jobs, the employer's need to keep them working, their ages, or any other criteria.[115]

But where the employer often accommodates injured employees, it likely must similarly accommodate pregnant employees.

For example, if an employee has an ADA qualified disability that renders them unable to lift heavy boxes or stand for long periods of time, then the employer would be required to make reasonable accommodations. Once the employer makes the accommodations, it likely will need to make the same accommodation for a pregnant employee who was unable to lift heavy boxes or stand for long periods of time.

---

[114] *Young v. United Parcel Service, Inc.*, 575 U.S. ___, 126 FEP Case 765, 775 (2015).
[115] *Id.* at 771.

D. Pregnancy Accommodation and the Hazardous Workplace

An employer is not required to accommodate a pregnant employee because the employee wants to protect her unborn child. While the U.S. Supreme Court has held that pregnant employees have the right to work in a hazardous environment,[116] there is no inverse rule requiring employers to provide on-the-job accommodations to employees who wish *not* to work in a hazardous environment. Furthermore, employees who have been denied requested accommodations to protect their unborn children have not been successful in court under the PDA.[117]

The leading case on this subject is *Armstrong v. Flowers Hospital, Inc.*[118] In *Armstrong*, a nurse brought a discrimination claim under the PDA because her employer refused to reassign her after she voiced concerns about treating an HIV-positive patient. The nurse, who had been concerned that caring for an HIV-positive patient would put her fetus at risk, claimed that the hospital's decision was unfairly applied to her. She also claimed, based on the U.S. Supreme Court's holding in *Johnson Controls*,[119] that the hospital's policy resulted in a disparate impact because it created a "difficult choice" for pregnant employees. The choice, she argued, between keeping her job or protecting her child, was prohibited by the U.S. Supreme Court.

The Eleventh Circuit rejected this argument. *Johnson Controls*, it stated, stood for the right of a pregnant employee, not the employer, to choose whether or not the employee continued in a particular job. The court further pointed out the limitations of pregnant employees' rights and the reasons why an employer has no duty to make alternative work available to pregnant employees: The PDA contains no language that addresses "the right of a pregnant employee, fully able to work, to receive benefits that are different from, and arguably superior to, the benefits available to other employees."[120]

---

[116] *Auto Workers v. Johnson Controls*, 491 U.S. 197 (1991). (Finding PDA violation where employer, fearful pregnant employee's unborn children will be harmed by exposure to toxins, banned fertile women from certain jobs).

[117] Calloway, Deborah. *Accommodating Pregnancy in the Workplace*, 25 Stetson L. Rev. 1, 36 (1995).

[118] 33 F.3d 1308 (11th Cir. 1994).

[119] Note 78, *supra*.

[120] *Armstrong*, 33 F.3d at 1316.

Furthermore, "employers can treat pregnant women as badly as they treat similarly affected but non-pregnant employees. Title VII simply does not require employers to treat their employees with kindness."[121]

Finally, a pregnant employee who finds herself facing the possibility of working in a potentially hazardous environment has three alternatives: continue working, seek a work situation with less stringent requirements, or leave the workforce. "In some cases, these alternatives may, indeed, present a difficult choice. But it is a choice that each woman must make."[122]

The court also dismissed the disparate treatment claim because the nurse had been unable to provide evidence that the hospital was treating her differently because of her pregnancy.

Although the case law does not lend support to a woman's desire to protect her fetus, there may be alternative methods of obtaining the desired outcome. One proposal holds that the best way to gain accommodation may be to demonstrate that the workplace hazard in question is harmful to the health of the pregnant woman herself.[123] If the ADA requires accommodations for individuals with disabilities who cannot perform physical labor or whose disabilities make them sensitive to toxins or who require frequent doctors' visits, then pregnant women who are similar in their ability to work and who require similar relief should, under the PDA, be entitled to the same accommodations.

---

[121] *Id.* at 1317.

[122] *Id.* at 1315.

[123] Calloway, Deborah, *Accommodating Pregnancy in the Workplace*, 25 Stetson L. Rev. 1, 38 (1995).

Chapter 6: The Right to Worker's Compensation

A. Generally

Officers and firefighters in the State of Washington are entitled to "no fault" accident and disability coverage, i.e. "worker's compensation," for injuries, occupational diseases, and deaths occurring in the course and scope of employment under the Industrial Insurance Act.[124] There are key differences between "injuries," and "occupational diseases."

The definition of "injury" under the statute is a "sudden and tangible happening, of a traumatic nature, producing an immediate or prompt result, and occurring from without, and such physical conditions as result therefrom."[125] Practically, an injury typically occurs as the result of an event or happening on a particular day that causes specific injuries, such as an assault, or a motor-vehicle collision on duty.

An "occupational disease," on the other hand, "is a disease or infection as arises naturally and proximately out of employment under the mandatory or elective adoption provisions of this title."[126] "Occupational diseases" do not include mental health conditions caused by stress, but do include conditions resulting from a sudden, tangible, and traumatic event that produces an immediate result.[127]

"Occupational diseases" generally occur over a period of time. For example, firefighters who are exposed to smoke, fumes, or toxic substances over a prolonged career may suffer respiratory diseases, cancer, or heart problems. Any of these particular conditions would be considered an "occupational disease" under the Industrial Insurance Act.

---

[124] Title 51, RCW.
[125] RCW 51.08.100.
[126] RCW 51.08.140, and *see City of Bellevue v. Raum*, 171 Wn. App. 124, 140 (2012).
[127] RCW 51.08.142; WAC 296-14-300(1)(stress caused by conflicts with a supervisor; actual or perceived threat of loss of a job, demotion, or disciplinary action; relationships with supervisors, co-workers, or the public; fear of exposure to chemicals, radiation biohazards, or other perceived hazards; objective or subjective stresses of employment; and personnel decisions); WAC 296-14-300(2); and *Rothwell v. Nine Mile Falls Sch. Dist.*, 149 Wn. App. 771, 780, 206 P.3d 347 (2009).

Employers may choose to pay premiums directly to the State, and have the State, through the Washington State Department of Labor and Industries (L&I), manage the worker's compensation claims and pay benefits. Instead of purchasing worker's compensation insurance coverage directly from the State, the employer can choose to self-insure. If an employer self-insures, the employee retains the same rights and benefits as those employees insured by the State, but the employer handles the paperwork generated as part of the claim, and pays benefits under the claim. A third-party administrator (TPA) is hired by the employer to manage the claims. However, L&I continues to handle any disputes arising under the claim.

Navigating the worker's compensation system can at times be frustrating and the challenges are sometimes greater when an employer is self-insured. Still the system is at least contemplated to be "user friendly" so that employees need not retain an attorney just because the employee suffers an on-the-job injury. At other times, when roadblocks are presented or the stakes are higher, legal counsel should be retained. This section Chapter attempts to describe how to navigate the system and identify when an employee might be better served having retained counsel.

B. Reporting an On-The-Job Injury Claim

If your members are injured on-the-job, the first step is to seek medical attention, if necessary.[128] Ordinarily, the health care provider who initially treats the on-the-job injury will provide the injured member with the Report of Accident (ROA) form. If not, the form is available online through the Department of Labor & Industries' website.[129] If the employer is self-insured, however, the injured worker will have to file the claim directly with the employer, or the TPA for the employer.

---

[128] An injured worker's first medical visit can be with any provider, hospital, or emergency room. However, after the first visit, the injured worker is required to select an attending provider through the Department's Medical Provider Network.

[129] *See* Report of Accident Form attached in Appendix ____.

The ROA initiates the worker's compensation claim. "Injury" claims must be filed within one year of the date of injury.[130] "Occupational disease" claims must be filed within two years following the date the worker had "written notice from a physician or a licensed advanced registered nurse practitioner: (a) [o]f the existence of his or her occupational disease, and (b) that a claim for disability benefits may be filed."[131]

The deadlines to file injury or occupational disease claims are firm. Worker's compensation claims will not be considered after the statutory deadline has expired. Make sure your members are aware of the deadlines involved to ensure the ROA is submitted in a timely manner.

After a ROA form has been submitted, the Department or self-insured employer decides whether to allow or deny the injury or occupational disease claim. To be covered under the Act, the "injury" must occur while the worker is acting in the course of employment."[132] Generally, if the employee is acting at the direction of his or her employer, or in furtherance of the employer's business, then the work is likely within the course and scope of employment.

Activities that are likely outside the scope of employment include the time an employee spends going to or coming from work; injuries that occurs in a parking lot; significant deviations from the route of travel;[133] and injuries occurring during work-sponsored sporting events.[134] Washington courts have also determined that emotional responses to traumatic events are allowable as industrial injuries under the Act.[135]

---

130 RCW 51.28.050.

131 RCW 51.28.055.

132 RCW 51.08.013.

133 Minor deviations from work are likely still within the scope of employment. *See, e.g.*, *In re Thomas Hart*, BIIA Dec., 35,767 (1971).

134 *See* RCW 51.08.13; *Puget Sound Energy, Inc. v. Adamo*, 113 Wn. App. 166, 462 P.2d 917 (1969); *Gray v. Department of Labor & Indus.*, 43 Wn.2d 578, 262 P.2d 533 (1953); and *In re Christopher Phillips*, BIIA Dec., 90 1386 (1991).

135 *Sutherland v. Department of Labor & Indus.*, 4 Wn. App. 333, 481 P.2d 453 (1971).

In the case of firefighters, certain occupational diseases are *presumptively* allowed. The value to a claimant of having a disease recognized as "presumptive" is that the burden of proof shifts to the employer to demonstrate that the disease is not work related. "Presumptive" diseases defined in the statute for firefighters include: (a) Respiratory diseases; (b) any heart problems, experienced within seventy-two hours of exposure to smoke, fumes, or toxic substances, or experienced within twenty-four hours of strenuous physical exertion due to firefighting activities; (c) cancer; and (d) infectious diseases (HIV/AIDS, all strains of hepatitis, meningococcal meningitis, or mycobacterium tuberculosis).

The Department or self-insured employer is allowed to rebut the presumptive allowance with evidence of the firefighter's "use of tobacco products, physical fitness and weight, lifestyle, hereditary factors, and exposure from other employment or nonemployment activities."[136] The cancer presumption only applies to firefighters who have worked for at least ten years, who were examined upon becoming a firefighter and found to not have cancer, and who only have certain types of cancer, including prostate cancer diagnosed prior to the age of fifty, primary brain cancer, malignant melanoma, leukemia, non-Hodgkin's lymphoma, bladder cancer, ureter cancer, colorectal cancer, multiple myeloma, testicular cancer, and kidney cancer.

In *Gorre v. City of Tacoma,*[137] a Tacoma firefighter lieutenant was able to show that his diagnosis of "Valley Fever" and his related respiratory symptoms presumptively qualified as an "occupational disease," and the lower courts mistakenly placed the burden on him to prove the existence of an occupational disease when in fact, the City had the burden to rebut the statutory presumption.

After a worker's compensation claim has been allowed, the injured employee will be assigned a claims manager who is the point-of-contact between the Department, or the self-insured employer. The claims manager will handle inquiries from the injured employee and any disputes that arise during the administration of the claim.

---

[136] RCW 51.32.185.

[137] *Gorre v. City of Tacoma* 180 Wn. App. 729, 324 P.3d 716 (2014).

C. Right to Medical Treatment

Once an industrial injury or occupational disease claim has been allowed, the Department or self-insured employer are legally obligated to pay for "proper and necessary medical and surgical services" provided by a physician or advanced registered nurse practitioner. The injured member is generally permitted to choose his or her own health care providers to treat their medical condition.[138] Medical treatment may include in-patient hospitalization, surgery,, out-patient medical care and rehabilitation, including physical therapy, , and prescription medications.

The Department ordinarily recognizes one attending medical provider on a claim. While the worker has a right to choose their own medical provider, the provider must be in the Department's Medical Provider Network.[139] Even though the Department's network of providers is fairly expansive, sometimes injured workers have difficulty finding health care providers who are willing to treat them because of the challenges in billing and receiving payment from the Department for covered services. Having a physician to not only treat the injured member, but also to advocate to the Department or self-insured employer on the injured member's behalf is very important.

D. Right to Time Loss and Loss of Earning Power Benefits

In addition to the right to medical treatment, the injured member also has a right to time loss compensation if he or she is temporarily unable to work as a result of an injury or occupational disease.[140] In order to qualify for time loss compensation, the injured member must provide a medical certification.

The time loss rate of compensation depends on the injured member's wages, marital status and number of dependents.[141] Cost of living adjustments are added onto the base time loss rate annually on July 1. The time loss rate is calculated based on the worker's wage of injury. The "daily wage" set by the Department may include shift differential, holiday pay, sick and vacation leave, and funeral leave.[142]

---

[138] RCW 51.36.010.

[139] *Id.*

[140] RCW 51.32.090(1).

[141] For a single officer with no children, the time loss rate is 60%. An additional 5% is added if married, and 2% is added for each child, up to a maximum of five children. *See* RCW 51.08.060(1).

[142] *See Fred Meyer, Inc. v. Shearer*, 102 Wn.App. 336, 8 P.3d 310 (2000) *review denied* at 143

While claim allowance and medical certification is ordinarily sufficient for entitlement to time loss compensation, there are particular circumstances where an injured member may be excluded from receiving such benefits. For example, an injured member may be ineligible for time loss benefits if his or her employer continues to pay the member's regular salary following the injury.[143] If the employer offers light duty work, and the medical provider releases the injured member to perform that work, then time lost benefits will be terminated regardless of whether the member accepts the job or not.[144] However, if the light duty assignment ends, but the injured member's provider does not believe he or she is able to return to his or her usual job, then time loss benefits will resume.[145]

An injured member may also be entitled to partial time loss benefits, or loss of earning power benefits, when the member is able to work in some form, but is earning less. This situation may arise where an officer or firefighter can perform a different job on a light duty basis that has a lower rate of pay. Such officer in that circumstance could be entitled to loss of earning power benefits.

The calculation of benefits owed to police and firefighters while an employee is on time loss is often misunderstood and miscalculated. LEOFF members have particular benefits that many public agencies simply either do not understand or ignore. In the next section, we explain the process for calculating the proper time loss compensation of an officer or firefighter.

E. Supplemental Benefits under LEOFF II

LEOFF I provided broad protection to public safety employees in the uniformed ranks of police officers and firefighters. LEOFF II significantly alters those protections. That is not a secret to anyone.

But the way the LEOFF II laws interact with workers compensation requirements still seems to be far more mysterious than it ought to over 30 years since the enactment of LEOFF II. There seems to be widespread noncompliance with the requirements of LEOFF II. Specifically, a number of jurisdictions are improperly applying the LEOFF II Supplement mandate.

Wn.2d 1003, 21 P.3d 290 (2000).

143 RCW 51.32.090(6).

144 RCW 51.32.090(4).

145 RCW 51.32.090(3).

In 1985, the legislature acted to address at least some of the equity issues that had been identified between LEOFF I and LEOFF II officers as to duty related injuries. They did this through the form of a "LEOFF II Supplement." The LEOFF II Supplement certainly does not entirely close the gap, but it does extend more coverage under workers compensation for police and firefighters injured at work than the law extends to any other covered class of employees.

The statute requires employers to provide for a period of 6 months, a "disability leave supplement." The supplement places the employee in the position of being able to maintain their wages. That supplement is defined in RCW 41.04.505:

> The disability leave supplement shall be an amount which, when added to the amount under RCW 51.32.090 [L&I Time Loss Payments] will result in the employee receiving the same pay he or she would have received for full time active service, *taking into account that industrial insurance payments are not subject to federal income or social security taxes.*[146]

There are two key aspects of this section that need to be interpreted and understood. First, is the notion of "same pay," which is neither defined in the regulations nor elsewhere in the law. Certainly, it means, at a minimum, that employees be paid the same base wage plus the applicable premiums the employee had before their on-the-job injury.

It is an open question about whether it requires continuation of other compensation such as deferred compensation. The statute does elsewhere require the continuation of "insurance benefits." But this clause would not seem to extend to benefits such as deferred compensation.

The second key requirement of this section is that employers are to bring the employee up to the same pay by "taking into account that the industrial insurance payments are not subject to federal income tax or social security taxes." This element seems clear enough, *but it seems to be often ignored by employers.*

[146] (Emphasis supplied.)

There is an extensive misunderstanding and misapplication of the LEOFF II Supplement among public employers and even employees, as well. It has been a practice of employers to take the entire check from L&I and then paying the employee their regular wage. Employees have been persuaded by payroll clerks that this is a “better way” to do it. It usually is explained to them that there is some type of benefit that they are receiving in this "better way.” Although when employees are later asked what the advantage is , usually they are unable to point to anything other than that they were able to maintain a regular paycheck and their benefits — to which they are entitled to anyway.

The only other enhancement that they get out of maintaining their position on the payroll is that they continue to accrue contractual leave benefits under the CBA. But whatever advantage this reaps, it is more than offset by the loss incurred by subjecting this to federal payroll tax. It is the tax consequences that are the most misunderstood and that have led to a misapplication of proper payment procedure. To see how, you have to consider how the disability supplement would be applied *if* the employer did not convert the L&I check.

Under RCW 41.04.510, employers are required to arrange for a “disability leave supplement.” This supplement is to be paid one-half out of the accrued paid leave of the employee, and the other half simply paid by the employer. The purpose of the disability leave supplement is to return the employee to the “same pay.”

This is obviously a disadvantage to an injured employee who ends up depleting their leave banks at a much faster rate than if the rules had been properly applied. In fact, in this example, and in many actual cases, the leave banks will deplete at twice the proper rate.

The employers do this, perhaps, for two possible reasons. First, it simply is “easier” for payroll people who do not have to make the painstaking calculations about what the net wage actually is supposed to be. Second, the employee, in fact, does deplete the leave banks quicker, meaning that the employer has less of an obligation to an employee who ends up with a long-term injury from which they cannot return after the LEOFF Supplement expires after 6 months. But from the officers perspective, during the midst of an injury is when you most need to preserve your leave banks.

There is another element of this program employees should be aware of, as well. The statute allows employees who are out long-term and covered by the disability supplement to "buy back" their credit so they can keep accruing retirement credit. *Employees must act affirmatively to obtain this benefit by contacting the Washington State Department of Retirement Systems once the period of disability begins.*

As of 2015, each LEOFF II employee contributes 8.41% of their gross earnings to their LEOFF II retirement pension. If the employee is injured and out on a period of disability, the employee may or may not have to buy back their service credits depending on the period of disability. An employee who is disabled for a period of 0-6 months will continue to accrue service credits, but will not have to "buy back" credits (even though the employer is obligated to do so). An employee who is disabled for 7-24 consecutive months, may buy back service credits at 8.41% per month, or at the applicable rate, for the period of disability. Unfortunately, employees who are out on disability leave for a period exceeding 24-consecutive months may not buy back service credits. However, if an employee is out on disability leave for 24-consecutive months, returns to work for a period of time, and then has a medical setback and is forced to take disability leave for another period, then the 24-month buy back period (with the same 6-month grace period) starts anew.

Employers sometimes sell employees on the notion that they get to continue accruing credit toward retirement when they are on full payroll status by turning over their L&I checks, but this is attainable anyway by the employee making direct arrangements to have the service credit payment made. While it may be somewhat more convenient to make this service credit through the regular payroll process, as demonstrated above, there is a potentially significant cost for this convenience.

Employers may (and have claimed) that they have a right to the L&I check. We have even seen instances where employers have pursued claims of "theft" against employees who sought to retain their L&I check. But, in fact, the law provides the employee every right to retain the check. L&I interpretations of the statute indicate an employer is prohibited from compelling employees to turn over their time-loss checks to "buy back" sick leave. On the other hand, an employer discharges its statutory obligations when it supplements these payments using sick leave and the LEOFF II supplement. Ultimately it is up to the employee to determine whether to retain the check and have it supplemented or to turn it over in exchange for salary.

F. Independent Medical Examinations

During the course of an industrial injury claim, the Department or self-insurer will likely request that the injured worker submit to an independent medical examination (IME). There is much controversy over whether these IMEs are truly "independent." Often the exams are conducted by physicians who are retired from practice, and who specialize in the particular area of medicine that relates to the specific injury or medical condition at issue.

The Department or self-insured employer will frequently order an injured worker to attend an IME when they disagree with the opinions of the worker's attending provider. However, even if the independent medical examiner offers a different opinion than the attending physician, "special consideration" is provided to the opinions and findings of attending physicians.[147] For good reason. Attending providers spend the most time with the worker and are most familiar with the injured worker's medical condition or conditions and related symptoms, treatment, and prognosis. Therefore, the attending provider's opinion should be afforded more weight than the opinion of the independent medical examiner who likely has only examined the worker on one occasion, for a very brief appointment.

While the process of preparing for and undergoing an IME can be stressful, the injured member cannot refuse to attend. If the worker does refuse to attend, the Department or self-insured employer can issue a "non-cooperation" order and stop paying time loss benefits. Once the Department or self-insured employer has scheduled an IME, if the injured worker has an attorney, the attorney should be consulted for advice prior to the IME. The following tips may also be useful:

- **Communication.** Once an IME is scheduled, the injured member should schedule an appointment with his or her attending provider to tell them the date of the IME, and the name of the examiner. The injured member should also tell their attending provider that after the IME, the Department or self-insured employer will likely send a form to the attending provider with a copy of the IME report. The form will ask the attending provider whether they "agree" or "disagree" with the findings of the examiner. *If they do not agree* with the

---

[147] *Hamilton v. Department of Labor & Indus.*, 11 Wn.2d 569 (1988).

findings or recommendations in the report, it is incumbent on the attending provider to explain *why* they disagree.

- **Honesty**. During the IME, be truthful, pleasant, and communicate directly and clearly with the examiner. The examiner is not only assessing the injured member's medical condition(s), ability to work, treatment, and the level of impairment, the examiner is also evaluating the credibility and likeability of the injured member.

- **Knowledge**. Understand the purpose of the IME and any potential biases the examiner may hold. If an examiner has conducted hundreds of IMEs, but has never (or very rarely) testified on behalf of an injured worker, then there is a significant likelihood the examiner may be biased.

G. Vocational Process

Unfortunately, an officer or firefighter may incur an injury so significant that a return to work duty is unlikely. At this point, the Department offers vocational rehabilitation services to help the employee find a new line of work.

Vocational rehabilitation services may also be extended to assist the injured member in returning to work in the same job. Early intervention services may be provided at the outset to assist the injured member in returning to work. These services may include helping the employer identify light-duty work, identifying and providing accommodations in the workplace, and/or completing workplace job analyses for the health care provider to review.[148]

Following any early intervention assessment, the Department or self-insured employer, may refer the injured member to an Ability to Work Assessment. This assessment is conducted by a vocational rehabilitation counselor (VRC) selected by the Department or self-insured employer. The purpose of the assessment is to determine whether the injured employee is "employable"[149] or requires vocational rehabilitation services. The assessment services may include:

---

[148] WAC 296-19A-050.

[149] WAC 296-19A-010 ("(a) 'Employable' means having the skills and training that are commonly and currently necessary in the labor market to be capable of performing and obtaining gainful employment on a reasonably continuous basis when considering the worker's: (i) Age, education, and experience; (ii) Preexisting

(1) Documenting work restrictions;
(2) Performing job analyses;
(3) Evaluating the worker's ability to work at the job of injury;
(4) Assessing transferable skills;
(5) Conducting labor market surveys as defined in WAC 296-19A-140;
(6) Evaluating the worker's ability to work at any other job;
(7) Evaluating the worker's ability to benefit from plan development services, including vocational testing if appropriate; and
(8) Assessing the worker's need for preferred worker status and when appropriate educating the worker on the preferred worker benefit.[150]

An important point to remember is that the job analyses created by the VRC (which describe the job of injury, each past job performed, other employment the worker can perform with his or her work skills, and any physical or mental health limitations) may be sent to *any* medical provider, who will determine whether the injured employee can perform the job duties associated with the job analyses. Prior to the medical provider's approval or disapproval, it is critically important for the injured member to request that his or her attending physician also review the job analyses to determine whether there are work skills or duties outlined in the analyses that are concerning to the worker.

Once the job analyses are submitted to the medical provider and approved or disapproved, several outcomes are possible.[151] First, if any of the job analyses are approved, a labor market survey will be conducted by the VRC to assess whether there are positions in the labor market that the injured worker can perform. If there are positions in the labor market that the injured worker can perform, then the VRC will conclude the worker is “employable” and will prepare a “closing report,” which is forwarded to the Department.

---

physical and mental limitations; and (iii) Physical and mental limitations caused, at least in part, by the worker's industrial injury or occupational disease. (b) Physical and/or mental conditions that arose after the industrial injury/occupational disease that were not caused or aggravated by the industrial injury/occupational disease are not considered in determining whether the worker is employable under the Industrial Insurance Act. (c) If there are no physical or mental restrictions caused by the worker's industrial injury/occupational disease, the worker must be found employable under the Industrial Insurance Act.”

[150] WAC 296-19A-065.

[151] WAC 296-19A-070.

Second, if the medical provider does not approve any of the job analyses, but the VRC concludes that vocational services are necessary and will likely enable the worker to become employable, then the VRC will probably determine that the worker is eligible for vocational rehabilitation plan development services.[152] This is not as common as an outcome as one might think. Indeed, few injured workers receive the benefits of plan development services because of the broad "employability" standard.

On the other hand, if the VRC concludes that the worker is not employable based on transferable skills and will not benefit from vocational rehabilitation plan development services, then the claim will most likely be forwarded to pension adjudicators for further review of whether the worker has a permanent disability.

During the vocational process, it is important to cooperate with the VRC. Having an attorney present during meetings with the VRC is strongly recommended. The VRC has no obligation to provide copies of the job analyses, assessment, or report to the injured member. Therefore, it is important for the worker to request these documents from the VRC to stay abreast of developments during the VRC process. Any disputes involving vocational issues are resolved by the Vocational Dispute Resolution Office at the Department.[153]

In the event an injured worker is referred for plan development services, the VRC will work with the employee to develop a rehabilitation plan.[154] Once the plan is approved, the injured worker has two options: Option 1: follow the Department's approved plan, or Option 2: develop his or her own plan.[155] At present, both plans offer the injured worker up to $17,599.11 for retraining (which is adjusted on July 1 each year).[156] Under Option 1, the employee only has two years for training, but continues to receive time loss and medical benefits while retraining. Under Option 2, the employee's claim is closed, and time loss and medical benefits end, but the employee is provided a vocational award equal to six months of time loss benefits. It is up to the injured worker to decide which option best suits their needs. However, Option 1 is highly recommended because if an employee is not fully retrained in six months, then it extends the time period for up to two years in which an employee can retrain while continuing to receive time loss and medical benefits.

---

[152] *Id.*

[153] WAC 296-19A-460.

[154] WAC 296-19A-090.

[155] WAC 296-19A-600-670 *et seq.*

[156] *See* http://www.lni.wa.gov/ClaimsIns/Claims/RTW/Training/Default.asp.

H. Claim Closure

1. Permanent Partial Disability

Once a workplace injury has reached "maximum medical improvement," the employee may be entitled to a permanent partial disability (PPD) award, which is a lump sum payment. The permanent partial disabilities are divided into two groups: specified and unspecified disabilities.[157] Once the disability is categorized in either of the two groups, the disability is given a rating or percentage of permanent impairment.[158] That rating is converted to compensation.[159] A PPD award is a lump sum paid at the conclusion of the claim.[160]

Often the Department or self-insured employer will hire an IME provider to evaluate the injured worker and rate the total PPD. Once that rating is provided, the worker and the attending provider should determine whether or not the rating is appropriate for the level of disability. It is not uncommon for an IME provider to find a lower or incorrect impairment rating than the rating identified by the injured worker's attending physician.

The attending physician has been treating the injured worker for much longer and is certainly more equipped to assess the level of impairment then an independent medical examiner who has likely only seen the injured worker on one occasion. As a result, to the extent the attending physician disagrees with the examiner, the injured worker has the option to challenge the rating.

The Department or self-insured employer will send an order and notice containing the PPD award. That notice will have appeal language as well as the deadline to appeal the PPD rating and award. If the attending provider and the worker do not agree with the rating and award, they should file a timely protest and request for reconsideration, or appeal with the Board of Industrial Insurance Appeals (BIIA), the appellate review board that hears appeals from Department decisions.

2. Reopening a Claim

---

157 WAC 296-20-19010, 19020.
158 RCW 51.32.080.
159 *Id.*
160 RCW 51.32.055.

Situations arise where an injured member had an open and allowed worker's compensation claim, receives treatment, ultimately recovers to the point of being able to return to work, the claim is closed, and then months, or years, later suffers an aggravation relating to the same initial injury. When this occurs, the injured member and his or her medical provider must submit a written application to reopen the prior claim.

The application must be submitted within 7 years from the date of the "first closure" of the claim.[161] Once the application is received, the Department has 90 days to act upon receipt of the written application to respond, or the application is deemed granted.[162] The Department or self-insured employer may extend the 90-day deadline for "good cause."[163]

In order to establish an aggravation, the worker must demonstrate, with medical testimony, a causal relationship between the injury and the subsequent disability,[164] "objective findings" that an aggravation of the injury resulted in increased disability,[165] the increased aggravation must have occurred between the respective terminal dates of the aggravation;[166] and the disability on the date of the order under appeal must be greater than the Department found it to be.[167] There are various types of aggravation cases, but most often they involve a worsening of a condition that is causally related to the worker's injury or occupational disease.

I. Protests and Appeals

---

[161] RCW 51.32.160. Technically, the first closing order is not final until 60 days have lapsed from the *receipt* of the order. Therefore, an injured worker may technically have 7 years plus 60 + days to file a reopening application.

[162] *Id.*

[163] *Id.*

[164] *Cyr v. Dept. of Labor & Indus.*, 47 Wn.2d 92 (1955).

[165] *Moses v. Dept. of Labor & Indus.*, 44 Wn.2d 511 (1954).

[166] The "terminal dates" are fairly complex, but generally the first terminal date is the last final order that previously closed the claim or denied the previous application to reopen, and the second terminal date is the date of the Department order under appeal. *See* WSAJ Worker's Compensation Deskbook.

[167] *Hyde v. Department of Labor & Indus.*, 46 Wn.2d 31 (1955).

Decisions by the Department or self-insured employer relating to the adjudication of worker's compensation claims must be communicated in writing to the injured worker.[168] Frequently these decisions are labeled "Order and Notice" or "Notice of Decision." Specific language is required by statute in these decisions.[169] Most importantly, the order must communicate the fact that the "order, decision or award" becomes final within "sixty days from the date the order is communicated to the parties."

Consequently, if the injured worker disagrees with the order, decision, or award, the worker has 60 days to file a "written request for reconsideration" with the Department or an appeal with the Board of Industrial Appeals (BIAA).[170] The BIAA will extend the time for filing one day if the 60th day falls on a weekend, or state holiday.[171]A request for reconsideration, or protest, must be in writing, but otherwise there are no specific requirements. An identification of the order at issue and a brief statement indicating what Department decision is being challenged or objected to will suffice.[172] Instead of filing a protest, the injured worker may also file an appeal with the BIAA. The Industrial Insurance Notice of Appeal form can be printed, completed, and delivered by mail, fax, or in person. The form can also be submitted online.[173] Upon receiving a protest or notice of appeal, the Department or self-insured employer may modify, reverse, or change any order, decision, or award, or hold the order, decision or award in abeyance for "a period of ninety days," which may be extended by the Department for "good cause."[174]

If the Department or self-insured employer does not modify or reverse the decision, then the appeal will progress through the administrative adjudicative process. At this point, if the injured member does not already have an attorney to represent their interests, the member should hire an attorney. While administrative hearings are slightly less formal than a civil or criminal trial, they have many similarities. An industrial appeals judge (IAJ) presides over the appeal hearing, and there are specific procedural and evidentiary rules that apply. Having an attorney who understands the process and the legal issues is essential to success on appeal.

---

[168] *See Rodriguez v. Department of Labor & Indus.*, 85 Wn.2d 949, 540 P.2d 1359 (1975).
[169] *See* RCW 51.52.050.
[170] *Id.*, and *see also* RCW 51.52.060.
[171] WAC 263-12-175.
[172] RCW 51.52.050.
[173] RCW 51.52.050-070, and WAC 263-12-10501. *See also* sample BIIA Notice of Appeal, attached as Appendix ___.
[174] RCW 51.52.060.

As far as the process on appeal is concerned, ordinarily, the BIIA will issue an "Order Granting Appeal" once it determines that it has jurisdiction over the matter. Once BIIA consents to jurisdiction, the parties (the injured worker and the Department and/or self-insured employer) will be contacted by a mediation judge to select a mediation conference date. At that stage, the parties or their legal counsel may discuss resolution prior to the conference. Prior to an adjudicative hearing, the parties may enter into an Order on Agreement of the Parties, which is essentially a settlement agreement to resolve the appeal.[175]

If there is an issue about a PPD rating, for example, the parties can also agree to a binding medical examination with a mutually agreed upon medical provider. While this is an option, it also places a lot of power and control in the hands of a physician who may or may not rule in favor the injured worker. As a result, binding examinations should not be utilized as a matter of course, but only when the provider selected is truly neutral and fair.

If the appeal is not resolved through mediation, an IAJ is assigned and a hearing will be scheduled. An initial pre-hearing conference will be held typically by telephone to discuss location and scheduling of the hearing, and deadlines related to discovery, witness confirmation, and depositions.

Often, medical providers are crucial witnesses in an injured member's case on appeal. However, medical providers are very busy, and may charge costly expert fees for their testimony. Fortunately, the BIIA permits witnesses to testify by "perpetuation deposition." Perpetuation depositions are testimonial and akin to providing live testimony at hearing.

While the course and scope of the hearing will be determined by legal counsel, it will likely include testimony from the injured member, family and friends of the injured member, medical providers, and/or a VRC. The Department or the employer will also have the opportunity to present their own witnesses, which may include medical experts, claims managers, a VRC, and coworkers or supervisors of the injured member. There is no perfect recipe for who will testify at hearing and ultimately that decision is up to the injured member's attorney, depending the facts of the particular case.

---

[175] WAC 263-12-093.

Once the hearing has concluded, the IAJ will issue a "Proposed Decision and Order."[176] If either party disagrees with the Decision and Order, they may file a Petition for Review (PFR) within 20-days of receipt of the Decision and Order to the BIIA.[177] The PFR is essentially a legal brief challenging the Decision and Order. If review is granted, the BIIA has 180 days from the date the PFR is filed to issue a final Decision and Order.[178]

If either party disagrees with the BIIA's final Decision and Order, or the BIIA denies the PFR, then the challenging party may appeal to Superior Court. If successful in Superior Court, the injured member's attorney may be entitled to attorney's fees and costs.[179] Similar to any civil court case, a final decision and order of the BIAA can be appealed from the Superior Court, to the Washington State Court of Appeals, and even to the Washington State Supreme Court.

J. Permanent Total Disability under the Industrial Insurance Act

Unfortunately, injuries occur in the workplace that render an injured member permanently and totally disabled from all work. "Permanent total disability" is statutorily defined as "loss of both legs, arms, or one leg and one arm, total loss of eyesight, paralysis or other condition permanently incapacitating the worker from performing any work at any gainful employment."[180] Most permanently disabled workers fall under the "other condition" category.

An injured worker is not required to be "absolutely helpless" or "physically broken and wrecked" to be permanently disabled under the IIA.[181] In determining whether an injured worker is "permanently disabled," the whole person is considered, which includes all pre-existing and other conditions, in addition to the condition caused by the workplace injury.[182] Nevertheless, the industrial injury or occupational disease must be a proximate cause of the disability rendering the worker unable to perform any gainful employment.[183]

---

[176] RCW 51.52.104, WAC 263-12-140, and WAC 263-12-150.

[177] WAC 263-12-145.

[178] WAC 263-12-145(4).

[179] RCW 51.52.130.

[180] RCW 51.08.160.

When the Department or self-insured employer determines that the injured member is permanently and totally disabled, the member is entitled to monthly disability pension payments for the remainder of their life. The amount of the monthly disability pension is determined by which option is selected by the injured worker. Option I allows the injured worker to receive the full extent of the benefits available during his or her lifetime, with benefits ending upon death.[184] Option II allows the injured worker to receive a reduced benefit, which, upon death continues and is paid to a surviving spouse, child, or other dependent.[185] Option III also provides for a reduced benefit, and upon death, one-half of the reduced benefit is paid to the surviving spouse, child, or other dependent.[186] Other federal and private programs are also available to the permanently disabled officer or firefighter, as set forth below.

---

[181] *Kuhnle v. Department of Labor & Indus.*, 12 Wn.2d 191, 197, 120 P.2d 1003 (1942).
[182] *Wendt v. Department of Labor & Indus.,* 18 Wn. App. 674, 682-83, 571 P.2d 229, 235 (1977).
[183] *Id.*
[184] RCW 51.32.067.
[185] *Id.*
[186] *Id.*

Chapter 7: Other Governmental Programs and Options for the Disabled Officer or Firefighter

Most public safety employees have financial and familial obligations that are significantly hampered by the loss of employment following a disabling injury. Other than the worker's compensation system, there are other governmental programs and private avenues for obtaining disability insurance benefits, including Social Security Disability, private disability insurance, and, for certain eligible employees, Public Safety Officers' Benefits. All of the various options should be explored to make sure that your permanently disabled members are receiving the full extent of the benefits they are entitled to.

A. Social Security Disability Insurance Benefits

1. Proof of Disability

A public safety employee who is permanently disabled from employment may qualify for Social Security disability benefits. A disabled member who is insured for disability insurance benefits, has not attained retirement age, has filed an application for disability insurance benefits, and is under a disability is entitled to Social Security disability benefits.[187] A "disability" is defined as:

> (A) inability to engage in any substantial gainful activity by reason of any medically determinable physical or mental impairment which can be expected to result in death or which has lasted or can be expected to last for a continuous period of not less than 12 months; or
>
> (B) in the case of an individual who has attained the age of 55 and is blind (within the meaning of "blindness" as defined in section 416 (i)(1) of this title), inability by reason of such blindness to engage in substantial gainful activity requiring skills or abilities comparable to those of any gainful activity in which he has previously engaged with some regularity and over a substantial period of time.[188]

---

[187] 42 U.S.C. § 423(a).
[188] *Id.*

In order to qualify for Social Security disability benefits, a disabled member must present evidence that his or her "physical or mental impairment or impairments are of such severity that he is not only unable to do his previous work but cannot, considering his age, education, and work experience, engage in any other kind of substantial gainful work which exists in the national economy...."[189] While proof of permanent disability is not easy, in awarding disability benefits, the Social Security administration considers the "whole person," including any overall physical, mental, or developmental impairments.

2. Application for Disability Benefits

An injured member who believes they are permanently disabled from performing "substantial gainful activity" as a result of a physical or mental impairment expected to last 12 or more months can apply for Social Security disability insurance benefits. These benefits can be applied for online, over the phone with a Social Security representative, or in person at their local Social Security office.

The application process can be fairly time-consuming and will likely require personal and work history information, and extensive medical background and history. The Social Security office might also require documentation to process the application including, a birth certificate; proof of citizenship; military discharge paperwork, W-2 forms or tax returns; medical evidence, such as doctor's reports, and test results; and/or paperwork related to any worker's compensation claims. Therefore, it is important to have this information available as part of the application process.

Once the application is submitted, an initial determination is made. Unless the disability is unquestionably severe, Social Security will frequently issue a denial upon the initial application. If a disabled member's initial application for Social Security is denied, it is a good idea to contact an attorney to guide the disabled member through the appeal process. Oftentimes, attorneys will not become involved in Social Security disability appeals, until after the first appeal, but beginning the process of researching and retaining an attorney early on is recommended.

[189] 42 U.S.C. § 423(d).

3. Appeal Process

There are technically four levels of appeal: reconsideration, hearing by an ALJ, review by the appeals council, and finally, federal court review. If the application is denied at the outset, the disabled member can request reconsideration of the adverse decision within 60-days of receipt of the denial.[190] This process can be done online at www.socialsecurity.gov/disability/appeal.

Depending on the reason for the initial denial, at this point, the injured member may be required to submit additional personal, employment, or medical information. If the request for reconsideration is denied, the injured member can request a hearing before an ALJ within 60 days of receiving the notice denying reconsideration.[191]

At this stage, having legal representation is critical. The hearing is the disabled member's opportunity to present evidence of disability. Frequently, Social Security will retain medical and vocational rehabilitation experts to testify at the hearings. As a result, having legal counsel to assist in preparing the injured member's case for hearing, which includes cross-examination of the experts retained by Social Security, is important to the success of the case.

If the disabled member is dissatisfied with the result at hearing, he or she can request Appeals Council review within 60 days of receiving the notice of the hearing decision or dismissal.[192] Appeals Council determinations can take a year or longer. If the Appeals Council issues a ruling adverse to the disabled member, he or she can request a civil action in federal district court within 60 days of the date the Appeals Council decision becomes final and judicially reviewable.[193]

4. Approval & Waiting Period

Once a Social Security disability claim is approved, the monthly benefit amount is determined and is payable on a monthly basis.[194] A five-month waiting period will generally be required before benefits are payable.[195]

---

[190] 42 U.S.C. § 405.
[191] 20 C.F.R. § 405.310.
[192] 20 C.F.R. § 404.968, and 405.401.
[193] 20 C.F.R. § 405.501.
[194] 20 CFR § 404.204, and 404.317.
[195] 42 U.S. Code § 423.

B. Private Disability Insurance Benefits

Many public safety employers will offer group short-and-long-term disability insurance benefits to its employees. The premium for disability insurance might be entirely employer-paid, or will be shared by the employee and the employer. Employer-paid plans are often governed by the laws of the Employee Retirement Income Security Act (ERISA).

Eligibility for disability benefits under these disability insurance plans are determined by the language of the insurance contract between the employer and the insurance carrier. The language defining "disabled" under these insurance contracts varies. Typical language defines "disability" during the first 24 months as being "unable to perform the material and substantial duties of his or her regular occupation" due to injury or sickness, or some variant of that language.[196] After 24-months, the definition of "disabled" is usually broadened, and a member may only be eligible for continued disability benefits if he or she is unable to perform, with reasonable continuity, the material and substantial duties of *any* occupation.

Again, this language varies in each plan, so if the member is covered under a disability insurance plan, the member should request a copy of the insurance plan from the employer or the insurer. Disability insurers will almost always require medical proof of disability.

A member who is temporarily or permanently disabled, is covered under a short-or-long-term disability insurance plan, applies for private disability benefits, and is subsequently denied benefits should consult with an attorney who specializes in private disability insurance appeals. Similar to the Social Security regulations, private disability insurance plans or policies also provide appeal rights. ERISA provides 180-days to appeal an adverse decision on a disability insurance claim.[197]

---

[196] *See e.g., Mitchell v. CB Richard Ellis Long Term Disability Plan*, 2010 U.S. App. LEXIS 27786 (9th Cir. 2010) (*unpublished*).
[197] 29 CFR § 2560.503-1.

Often, law enforcement or fire unions sponsor disability plans, either directly or through statewide councils with which they affiliate. Sometimes these plans are paid in part or whole by the employer under the terms negotiated in the CBA. Sometimes they are paid entirely by the members.

There are some tax implications involved with these plans that should be considered when they are established, especially as to the issue of whether you want to negotiate to have the employer pay the premium. The taxation of disability insurance and benefits is a bit complicated, and public safety unions and their members should make some thought-out choices on this subject. *One way or the other, the income associated on such a benefit is going to be taxed, and you have to decide the best way to face that tax.*

If the employer pays for the premium, the insurance *premium* is a tax free benefit, but in an instance in which an individual disability is later incurred, and benefits are paid out, the *payout* will then be treated as taxable income. On the other hand, if the employees pay for the premium out of their already taxed wages, a later insurance payout is exempt from taxation.

A different rule applies where the employer, as often is the case, pays for only a portion of the disability insurance premium. In that instance, the benefit is taxed on a "pro rata" basis: The proportion of the premium paid by the employee's post-tax contribution is exempt from tax, and the proportion that was paid as a benefit by the employer is subject to tax.

There is an element of choice, of course here. But generally when we explain the options and tax implications to clients, many make the election to forego putting their total compensation dollars into employer paid disability in favor of other paid benefits and member-paid disability premiums.

C. Public Safety Officers' Benefits Act: Death, Disability, and Education Assistance Benefits

1. Death and Permanent Disability Benefits

The Public Safety Officers' Benefits Program provides a one-time payment of $339,881 (as of February 4, 2016, and adjusted annually) to families of public safety officers who die (on or after September 29, 1979) or are permanently and totally disabled (on or after November 29, 1990) as a "direct and proximate result of a personal injury sustained in the line of duty."[198] If there is no children, the entire benefit is paid to the spouse.[199] If there is a spouse and one child, the benefit is split 50-50 between the spouse and the child.[200] If there is a spouse and more than one child, or no spouse, and multiple children, the payment is split between the spouse and children, or the children in equal shares.[201] In the event the member has no spouse or children, the benefit is paid to other designated beneficiaries or to the member's parents.

The PSOBA defines "public safety officer" as an individual serving in a public agency (state or local) in an official capacity with or without compensation as a law enforcement officer, firefighter, or chaplain; an employee of the Federal Emergency Management Agency who is performing official duties related to a major disaster or emergency; a State, local or tribal employee who is performing official duties in cooperation with FEMA; and a member of a rescue squad or ambulance crew who is engaging in rescue activity or emergency medical services.[202] The definition of "law enforcement officer" covers any individual involved in crime and juvenile delinquency control or reduction, or enforcement of the criminal law, including, police, corrections, probation, parole, and judicial officers.[203]

The scope of which employees are, or are not, covered has been the subject of some litigation. An EMT designated as an "associate firefighter" has been determined to fall within the scope of PSOBA's coverage.[204] But private fire pilots have been held to be excluded.[205] In *Moore v. Department of Justice*,[206] the U.S. Court of Appeals for the Federal Circuit similarly held that eight firefighters who were killed in an accident as they drove home from fighting a forest fire were not "public safety officers" because they were employed by a private company.

---

[198] *See* Public Safety Officers' Benefit Act of 1976 (PSOBA), 42 U.S.C. § 3796(a).
[199] *Id.*
[200] *Id.*
[201] *Id.*
[202] 42 U.S.C. § 3796b (9).
[203] 42 U.S.C. § 3796b (4).
[204] *Winuk v. United States*, 2007 U.S. Claims Lexis 199, 77 Fed. Cl. 207 (2001).
[205] *Groff v. U.S.*, 2007 U.S. App. Lexis 15821 (Fed. Cir.).
[206] 760 F.3d 1369 (2014).

In *Cassella v. United States*, [207] the Federal Circuit court disallowed PSOBA coverage for a noncommissioned "school zone officer." The officer was regulating traffic wearing a department-issued police vest. The evidence indicated that the officer had no arrest or criminal citation authority, but was responsible for safeguarding children crossing streets. The court held she was not covered because the Act only applied to "law enforcement officers" empowered to enforce the criminal, not civil laws.

The Act limits recovery to deaths that arise "in the line of duty." This issue has been intensely contested at times and the Department of Justice that administers the benefits has often applied a restrictive definition of the "line of duty" requirement. These DOJ restrictive interpretations have frequently been criticized by the federal courts that have overturned benefit denials and applied a broader eligibility definition. Courts have held that PSOBA should be "applied liberally,"[208] something that DOJ has not consistently done. Under the PSOBA, a heart attack, stroke, or vascular rupture suffered by a public safety officer and causing death is a presumptive personal injury if:

> (1) [T]he public safety officer, while on duty—
>
> (A) engages in a situation involving nonroutine stressful or strenuous physical law enforcement, fire suppression, rescue, hazardous material response, emergency medical services, prison security, disaster relief, or other emergency response activity; or
>
> (B) participates in a training exercise involving nonroutine stressful or strenuous physical activity;
>
> (2) [T]he heart attack, stroke, or vascular rupture commences—
>
> (A) while the officer is engaging or participating as described in paragraph (1);
>
> (B) while the officer remains on that duty after being engaged or participating as described in paragraph (1); or
>
> (C) not later than 24 hours after the officer is engaged or participating as described in paragraph (1); and

[207] 469 F.3d 1376 (Fed. Cir. 2006).
[208] *Demutiis v. United States*, 48 Fed. Cl. 81 (2000), affirmed in part and modified in part on other grounds at 291 F.3d 1373 (Fed. Ct. 2002).

(3) [T]he heart attack, stroke, or vascular rupture directly and proximately results in the death of the public safety officer...[209]

This presumption can be rebutted with competent medical evidence establishing that the heart attack, stroke, or vascular rupture was "unrelated to the engagement or participation or was directly and proximately caused by something other than the mere presence of cardiovascular-disease risk factors."[210]

The Federal Circuit in *Greeley v. U.S.* held that the death of a volunteer firefighter from a fatal heart attack, suffered after extinguishing a fire in the basement of a building, was not within the scope of the PSOBA.[211] The Circuit Court held that the firefighter's widow was unable to establish that a traumatic injury was the cause of the firefighter's death, or that an injury was a substantial factor in his death, since the widow presented no evidence that smoke inhalation, carbon monoxide intoxication, or other acute injury occurred, and her own medical experts conceded that there was no indication in the autopsy that her husband had experienced traumatic injury.[212]

In *Durco v. U.S.*,[213] the Federal Claims Court denied survivor benefits to the widow of a volunteer firefighter whose death, the Court determined, was caused by atherosclerotic cardiovascular disease and his brief exposure to cold weather was not a "traumatic injury" which directly and proximately caused his death. The Federal Claims Court also denied benefits to the widow of another volunteer firefighter in *North v. U.S.*[214] who was unable to present evidence that her husband suffered smoke or carbon monoxide inhalation, or sustained a personal injury prior to his death, or that a personal injury contributed in any way to his death so as to render it compensable.

PSOBA Benefits are not available if the member's death or injury was caused by intentional misconduct; suicide; the member was voluntarily intoxicated at the time of the injury or death; the member was performing his or her duties in a grossly negligent manner at the time of the injury or death; the beneficiary of the benefit caused the injury or death to the member; or to military personnel.[215]

---

209 42 U.S.C. § 3796(k)

210 *Id.*

211 50 F.3d 1009 (Fed. Cir. 1995).

212 *Id.*

213 14 Cl. Ct. 424, 1988 WL 20507 (1988).

214 1 Cl. Ct. 93, 555 F. Supp. 382 (1982).

215 42 U.S.C. § 3796a, Sec. 1202.

In *Yanco v. United States*,[216] the court disallowed coverage for a Massachusetts police officer whose on-duty work eventually led to emotional distress that led him to commit suicide. The court held that the statute specifically disallowed emotional stress and suicide from the scope of the statutory benefit.

Federal courts have interpreted "line of duty" to include job-related coming to and going from work. In *Russell v. Law Enforcement Assistance Administration*,[217] the Ninth Circuit held that the widow of a police sergeant who died in a car accident while returning home from work was entitled to death benefits because he was required to use his own car on the job, he typically spent much of his workday on the road, he used his car for job-related activities on the day of the accident, when driving home he was rendering service to his employer by transferring a piece of law enforcement equipment, and as a weekend duty detective he had to put in long hours, and was driving home at a particularly dangerous time, late on Saturday night, when he was killed.

PSOBA claims for death benefits must be filed within three years of the public safety officer's death or injury, or within one year after a final determination of entitlement to receive, or of denial of, the benefits.[218] The PSOBA benefit is available in addition to any other benefit from any other source, and prohibits the States from offsetting any state-funded death benefits against the PSOBA benefits.[219] In *Rose v. Arkansas State Police*,[220] the U.S Supreme Court invalidated an Arkansas workers compensation law that attempted to create an offset for PSOBA benefits.

---

[216] 258 F.3d 1356 (Fed. Cir. 2001).
[217] 637 F.2d 1255 (9th Cir. 1980).
[218] 28 C.F.R. §§ 32.12(a), and 32.22(a).
[219] **42 U. S. C. § 3796(e)**, and *see also Rose v. Arkansas State Police*, 479 U.S. 1, 3-4, 107 S. Ct. 334 (1986).
[220] 479 U.S. 1 (1986).

If a death or disability benefit claim is denied, the claimant may move for reconsideration of the denial.[221] However, in order to exhaust his or her administrative remedies, the claimant must request a Hearing Officer determination, before filing a civil lawsuit for relief. This request must be filed within 33 days of the denial of the claim.[222] If the Hearing Officer affirms the denial, the claimant must appeal to the Director of the PSOB Office no later than 33 days after service of the denial.[223] If the Director denies the PSOB claim, the claimant may then pursue a civil claim in court. Given the amount at stake and the sometimes restrictive view DOJ has taken on benefits, families would be well-served by consulting with legal counsel before presenting such a claim.

In addition to the PSOBA, retirement contributions of a deceased member are also a death benefit available to the surviving spouse, domestic partner, child, or the estate of a deceased member under Washington law.[224] The "Behind the Badge Foundation" is a good resource available to Washington law enforcement agencies and members for providing information and support in the event of a line of duty death.[225]

2. Educational Assistance

The PSOBA also provides educational assistance[226] to family members of public safety officers who die or are totally and permanently disabled in the line of duty.[227] The educational assistance provided is a monthly allowance for students in full-time, three-quarter-time, or half-time education programs.[228] Subject to certain limitations, a claim for educational assistance may be filed with the PSOB Office at any time after the injury date.[229] Similar to the death and disability benefit, if a claim for educational assistance is denied, the claimant must request a Hearing Officer determination before pursuing any civil claims in court, then must appeal to the Director.[230]

---

[221] 28 C.F.R. § 32.27.
[222] 28 C.F.R. §§ 32.27, 32.29, and 32.42.
[223] 28 C.F.R. § 32.52.
[224] RCW 41.04.393 and 41.26.510.
[225] http://behindthebadgefoundation.org/
[226] "Educational assistance" includes expenses for tuition and fees, room and board, computer equipment, supplies, and transportation. 28 C.F.R. §§ 32.33.
[227] 42 U.S.C. § 3796d-1.
[228] 38 U.S.C. § 3532.
[229] 28 C.F.R. § 32.32.
[230] 28 C.F.R. §§ 32.37, and 32.55.

D. Offsets & Overpayments

Once a public safety officer is receiving disability benefits from multiple sources, the issue of offsets and overpayments arises. Social Security, L&I, and most private disability insurance contracts often have statutory or contractual language permitting them to offset any amount paid in disability benefits by the amount of benefits received from other sources. For example, if Social Security determines that a claimant is entitled to a set monthly benefit amount, but the agency determines that the employee is also receiving monthly pension benefits through worker's compensation, and/or long-term disability benefits, then Social Security is permitted to *deduct* the amount received from other sources from the monthly Social Security benefit.

Unfortunately, permanently disabled employees often are unaware of the "right of offset," and will accept the full extent of benefits from each source. When that occurs, the disabled employee has received an "overpayment," which he or she will then have to *pay back* to whichever source was entitled to the offset. Sometimes, a disabled member may be receiving disability benefits for months or years, and then learns a huge overpayment has been assessed. An overpayment can be stressful and life-altering when finances are tight.

Determining which source of disability benefits is entitled to an offset is extremely complicated, but the best way to avoid an overpayment is to *communicate* with each source to make sure that they are all aware of the full extent of disability benefits received through each source. While it may seem very beneficial to be receiving a higher benefit amount (especially when, after receiving disability benefits from all sources, the officer or firefighter may still not be receiving the same amount of compensation they were receiving prior to being permanently disabled), the long-term ramifications of not communicating with each source, e.g., a significant overpayment, can be potentially devastating to the disabled member and his or her family.

Chapter 8: The Right to a Safe Workplace: Labor and Industry Rules for Law Enforcement Officers and Firefighters

A. Occupational Health & Safety Standards in Washington

The federal Occupational Health and Safety Act (OSHA) is a comprehensive statute intended to protect employees from occupational health and safety hazards in the workplace.[231] OSHA applies to employers "engaged in a business affecting commerce who has employees, but does not include the United States (not including the United States Postal Service) or any State or political subdivision of a State."[232]

Most law enforcement officers and firefighters are employed by the State, or a political subdivision of the State, and are *not* subject to the OSHA standards. Fortunately, Washington State has created its own health and safety regulations, the Washington Industrial Safety and Health Act (WISHA), which applies to the State, and all of the counties, cities, and municipal corporations in Washington.[233] The Division of Occupational Safety and Health (DOSH) is part of the Washington Department of Labor and Industries. DOSH is responsible for developing and enforcing health and safety rules, and providing employers with on-site consultations to assist in facilitating safe workplaces.

[231] 29 U.S. Code § 651.
[232] 29 U.S. Code § 652 (5).
[233] RCW 49.17.020 (4).

Under WISHA, each employer in Washington is responsible for providing his or her employees with "a place of employment free from recognized hazards that are causing or likely to cause serious injury or death to his or her employees" and is obligated to comply with WISHA's "rules, regulations, and orders."[234] In fact, WISHA gives the State the right to enter the premises of any covered employer who is believed to be in violation of the Act.[235] If a violation is found, the State may issue citations, seek restraining orders, [236] order civil and criminal penalties,[237] and, in limited circumstances, may order an employer to pay damages to employees injured as a result of the employer's failure to comply with WISHA safety regulations.

B. Special Rules for Firefighters

The Department of Labor & Industries in accordance with WISHA has adopted specific safety and health standards applicable to firefighters and employees specialized to work in a fire brigade.[238] The rules are fairly broad in scope and address many health and safety issues, including, but not limited to, injury and illness reporting;[239] accident/incident investigation;[240] first-aid training and certification;[241] personal protective equipment and protective clothing;[242] respiratory equipment protection;[243] incident management;[244] fire suppression;[245] occupational exposure to heat and cold stress;[246] technical rescue training,[247] standard operating procedures,[248] response planning,[249] equipment,[250] and safety;[251] and wildland fire operations.[252] A complete list of Washington's firefighting safety rules and regulations can be found online.[253]

---

[234] RCW 49.17.060.
[235] RCW 49.17.070.
[236] RCW 49.17.120, and 49.17.130.
[237] RCW 49.17.180 and 49.17.190.
[238] WAC 296-305-01001 *et seq.*, and 296-811-100 et seq.
[239] WAC 296-305-01501.
[240] WAC 296-305-01503.
[241] WAC 296-305-01515.
[242] WAC 296-305-02001, and WAC 296-800-160. *See also* WAC 296-305-02002-02012.
[243] WAC 296-305-04001.
[244] WAC 296-305-05000.
[245] WAC 296-305-05002.
[246] WAC 296-305-05004.
[247] WAC 296-305-05103.
[248] WAC 296-305-05105.
[249] WAC 296-305-05107.
[250] WAC 296-305-05109.
[251] WAC 296-305-05111.
[252] WAC 296-305-07001.
[253] http://apps.leg.wa.gov/WAC/default.aspx?cite=296-305.

In addition to the WISHA standards, the National Fire Protection Association (NFPA) has published its own workplace standards for firefighters and those engaged in fire protection activities. NFPA standards govern station/work uniforms for fire and emergency services, protective equipment for proximity and structural firefighting, ballistic resistance body arm, and Personal Alert Safety Systems. The NFPA standards are considered the gold standard in firefighter safety.

C. General Standards for Law Enforcement

Specific standards have not been developed for other public safety employees, including law enforcement officers. That does not mean that there are not safety rules that apply to employers. Instead, the employers are subject to the general safety rules applicable to all occupations including those in Chapters 296-24,296-62, and 296-800 of the Washington Administrative Code.

A recurring issue that arises in law enforcement and corrections work concerns the safety hazards arising from understaffing. L&I has not exercised authority to identify understaffing as a citable safety violation. L&I has investigated and sometimes cited employers for violations concerning failed communication systems.

D. Safety Complaints

An employee who believes that his or her employer has committed a health and safety violation, should immediately report it to the Department of Labor & Industries. A fillable safety complaint form can be downloaded from the L&I Website.[254]

Experience indicates that L&I takes safety complaints seriously and investigates them, usually by coming on-site. The safety investigator normally allows the union representative to be present during safety inspections and communicates the results of investigations after it is completed.

---

254 http://www.lni.wa.gov/FormPub/Detail.asp?DocID=1784

E. Whistleblower Retaliation

An employer may not discharge or discriminate against an employee who complains about a workplace health and safety issue, or testifies or may testify in a proceeding involving a health and safety complaint or violation.[255] An employee who believes that he or she has been discharged or discriminated against for complaining about workplace health and safety violations, may within *thirty days* after the violation occurs, complain to DOSH.[256] The Director must make a decision regarding the complaint within 90 days.[257] If the Director determines that a WISHA violation has occurred, he or she shall bring a civil court action against the employer.[258] If the Director determines that no WISHA violation has occurred, then the employee may file a lawsuit within *30 days.*[259] The time frame for bringing the initial complaint and filing suit is very short. Therefore, a police officer or firefighter who believes they have been discharged or discriminated against for reporting workplace safety violations, should immediately report it to DOSH.

---

255 RCW 49.17.160.

256 *Id.*, and *see* attached Discrimination Complaint form.

257 RCW 49.17.160(3).

258 *Id.*

259 *Id.*

Chapter 9: Civil Claims for Workplace Injuries

The various income protection programs we have identified so far are designed, as much as possible, to help your injured and disabled members bridge to a new occupation while affording some level of income security. No doubt, these programs are valuable, but let's not be mistaken here: For most public safety employees, these programs do not even come close to making the employee (or former employee) whole for what they have suffered.

While not available in all cases, the civil justice system does sometimes afford additional remedies that may allow your members to reach closer to being "made whole." Depending on the circumstances, a legal claim may exist that could be brought either against the employer or the third party responsible for an injury. This chapter explores both avenues.

A. Potential Claims against the Employer

Washington police and firefighters have been extended important civil litigation rights in connection with their workplace injuries that are often not well-understood, even by the private attorneys that might be assisting them. These rights provide an important means to help make these employees whole in ways that the workers compensation system does not. In fact, we have come to recognize that there is widespread misunderstanding or ignorance about the ability of Washington police and firefighters to bring claims against their employer.

The extent to which a Washington public safety employee may bring a legal civil claim against the employer is impacted dramatically by whether or not the employee is covered by LEOFF. In general, an employer covered under the IIA is immune from civil suit for workplace injuries arising out of the employer's negligence.[260] This form of employer "immunity" was a key consideration in the original design of the workers compensation system. A "quid pro quo" was applied which offered the employees relief for their injuries without the need to bring legal claims while offering employers protections against those legal claims. This was described by the Washington Supreme Court:

> Washington's IIA was the product of a grand compromise in 1911. Injured workers were given a swift, no-fault compensation system for injuries on the job. Employers were given immunity from civil suits by workers.[261]

The limitation on suits arising from employer negligence does not bar all lawsuits. Despite the IIA immunity an employer may be sued when it committed an intentional physical injury, or if the employer had actual knowledge that an injury was certain to occur and willfully disregarded that knowledge.[262] This exception to the general employer immunity rule is set forth in RCW 51.24.020:

> If injury results to a worker from the deliberate intention of his or her employer to produce such injury, the worker or beneficiary of the worker shall have the privilege to take under this title and also have cause of action against the employer as if this title had not been enacted, for any damages in excess of compensation and benefits paid or payable under this title.

Non-LEOFF public safety employees subject to this IIA immunity have nonetheless, from time-to-time, prevailed on civil claims by proving their injuries were a result of the "deliberate" actions of their employer. Establishing such claims is not easy. Even "gross negligence" on the employer's party does not cause them to lose their immunity.[263] The employee would have to demonstrate not that the employer's actions were intentional but rather that the employer intended the actual injury.[264] The courts have held, though, that this standard is met when the employee can prove that the employer had actual knowledge that an injury was certain to occur and "willfully disregarded" that knowledge.

---

[260] RCW 51.04.010).

[261] *Birklid v. Boeing Company*, 127 Wn.2d 853, 904 P.2d 278 (1995).

[262] *Birklid v. The Boeing Co.*, 127 Wn.2d 853, 865, 904 P.2d 278 (1995); *see also Walston v. Boeing Co.*, 181 Wn.2d 391, 399 (2014) (employee could not pursue claims against his employer outside of workers' compensation when he could not show that the employer deliberately injured him or had actual knowledge of certain injury resulting from asbestos exposure).

[263] *Nielson v. Wolfkill Corp.*, 47 Wn. App. 352, 734 P.2d 961 (1987).

[264] *Id.*

A recent example of this type of claim is presented in the still pending case of WSP Trooper Michelbrink who brought suit claiming that the State Patrol had caused his deliberate injury during Taser training. Trooper Michelbrink suffered severe pain from a Taser barb and was afterwards diagnosed with a fractured vertebrae and bulged disc, which he claimed was a result of the Taser training.

The trial court denied the State Patrol's dismissal motion and that ruling was upheld by the Court of Appeals.[265] The court rejected the WSP defense that the injury was part of a training regime. It also rejected the argument that the WSP did not have certain knowledge that a serious injury would result. It explained that it was well-documented that Taser training was likely to cause *some* pain and minor injury and that knowledge was sufficient to remove the Patrol from IIA immunity. The Supreme Court granted review and remanded the case back to the Court of Appeals. The Court of Appeals reversed its prior holding that the "deliberate intention exception should be liberally interpreted," but narrowly applied the exception to the case and held that there were genuine issues of material fact as to whether WSP had actual knowledge that an injury was certain to occur from Taser exposure and as to whether WSP willfully disregarded that knowledge.[266] As a result, Trooper Michelbrink's claims against WSP survived.

Law enforcement officers and firefighters covered under LEOFF, though, are not subject to such narrow recourse. When the LEOFF (LEOFF I) statute was adopted, police and firefighters were completely exempted from the workers compensation system. When LEOFF II was enacted, LEOFF II personnel not only lost the broader health and disability coverage of the LEOFF I system, but they were also placed into the Workers Compensation system. Fortunately, a right to sue exemption was established in RCW 41.26.280.

---

265 180 Wn. App 656, 323 P.3d 620 (2014), review granted, 180 Wn.2d 1028 (2014).

266 *Michelbrink v. Wash. State Patrol*, 2015 Wash. App. LEXIS 2912 (2015).

Under RCW 41.26.280, if injury or death results to a law enforcement officer or firefighter LEOFF member[267] from the intentional or negligent act or omission of a governmental employer, the officer or firefighter, or his or her widow, widower, child, or dependent has a cause of action against the governmental employer for any *excess* damages over the amount received or receivable from worker's compensation.[268] Essentially, this exception allows law enforcement officers or firefighters injured or killed in the line of duty to pursue a civil action against his or her government employer for any damages that exceed the amount of worker's compensation benefits received. Worker's compensation typically falls short of fully compensating the injured worker for his or her injuries, and medical expenses, and provides no monetary damages for emotional distress.

To the extent a law enforcement officer or firefighter is successful in a civil lawsuit against their governmental employer, any judgment, verdict or settlement that is received will be offset by the amount received by worker's compensation. However, the Department or self-insured employer is not entitled to an offset or deduction for loss of consortium or noneconomic damages (such as emotional distress) because they are not paying those types of benefits under the worker's compensation claim.[269]

Firefighters and officers have successfully pursued negligence claims against their departments in a number of situations:

- Redmond officer who was shot in foot by fellow officer;[270]
- Spokane County deputy who suffered head injuries incurred during fight with suspect when backup called off;[271]
- Seattle firefighter who suffered severe injuries from fall down fire station hole retains $12.75 million dollar verdict;[272]

[267] RCW 41.26.030 defines who qualifies as a "law enforcement officer" or "firefighter" under the LEOFF statute.

[268] *See* RCW 41.26.281, *Fray v. Spokane County*, 134 Wn.2d 637, 952 P.2d 601 (1998), and *Locke v. City of Seattle*, 162 Wn.2d 474, 485, 172 P.3d 705 (2007).

[269] *Tobin v. Department of Labor & Industries*, 169 Wn.2d 396, 239 P.3d 544 (2010)*Flanigan v. Department of Labor & Industries*, 123 Wn.2d 418, 869 P.2d 14 (1994).

[270] *Taylor v. City of Redmond*, 89 Wn.2d 315, 517 P.2d 1388 (1977).

[271] *Fray v. Spokane County*, 134 Wn.2d 637, 952 P.2d 601 (1998).

[272] *Jones v. City of Seattle*, 179 Wn.2d 322, 314 P.3d 380 (2013).

- Kennewick officer who was injured during hazardous driving training;[273]

- Pierce County deputy who was hit by another deputy's car during foot pursuit;[274]

- Seattle trainee firefighter who was injured in fall from 50 foot ladder, court rejected claim that "trainees" were not covered by LEOFF requirements;[275]

- Seattle horse patrol officer who suffered severe injuries in fall from his service horse and later died.[276]

When a workplace injury is caused by the negligence or intentional actions of the employer, the union representative can help guide the injured officer or firefighter. There are numerous resources available to the injured officer or firefighter, but one important resource is the union attorney. The union attorney likely has experienced litigators able to handle any claims and lawsuits against the employer or help identify qualified legal counsel for them. If, for some reason, the union attorney is unable to assist the injured officer or firefighter in locating counsel, then in addition to referrals from family and friends, the Washington State Association for Justice (formerly the Washington Trial Lawyers' Association) is a great place to start in finding a competent attorney.

Make sure to find an attorney who handles similar cases, and make sure your injured members meet with more than one attorney to find the right attorney for their case. In addition to the ROA form filled out for the Department, the public safety employer may also have reporting procedures when workplace injuries occur. To be an effective union advocate, the union representation should familiarize himself or herself with the employer reporting procedures and guidelines.[277]

---

[273] *Lascheid v City of Kennewick*, 137 Wn.App 633, 154 P.3d 207 (2007), review denied 164 Wn,2d 1037, 197 P.3d 1185 (2008).
[274] *Beaupre v. Pierce County*, 161 Wn.2d 568, 166 P.3d 712 (2007).
[275] *Locke v. City of Seattle*, 162 2d. 474, 172 P.3d 705 (2007).
[276] *Lindell v. City of Seattle* (consolidated with *Locke v. City of Seattle*), 162 2d. 474, 172 P.3d 705 (2007).
[277] These policies are often contained in the general policies, the department-specific policies, or even in Lexipol.

B. Claims Against a Third Party

An injured worker may also pursue a lawsuit against third parties who are not the employer.[278] Injuries caused by third parties are not uncommon for public safety officers, and often occur when officers or firefighters are at the scene of an incident, or driving in their department-issued vehicles.

Historically suits against third parties have been somewhat restricted by what has been known as the "professional rescue doctrine" or what was also known in earlier form as the "fireman's rule." Under this common law doctrine, courts restricted liability when police or fire responded to an emergency on the theory that their professional response involved an "assumption of risk" that they were paid to incur.

Over time, the courts have restricted this doctrine. This doctrine, though, still restricts liability for injuries resulting from the direct emergency for which the officer or firefighter is responding. An example of the potentially harsh impact of the doctrine was demonstrated in a lawsuit brought by the family of deceased Tacoma Officer Bill Lowry.

Lowry and Tacoma officers had assisted the Auburn Police Department in a high risk SWAT operation. Lowry was killed when the suspect shot him with his AK-47 assault rifle. The Court of Appeals disallowed the Lowry family's claim, reasoning that under the "professional rescue doctrine," Lowry's death was a direct result of the threat that he was responding to, distinguishing other cases in which the injury was *independent* of the reason for the initial response. The court concluded: "In summary, because Lowry assumed the risks inherent in the job of being a SWAT Team officer, the professional rescuer doctrine precludes the Lowrys from collecting damages."[279]

But courts have made it clear that this doctrine does not apply to preclude recovery from injuries caused by third parties independent of the initial emergency. For instance courts have allowed claims for:

---

[278] RCW 51.24.030(1). If the injured employee elects not to personally pursue his or her third party claim, the Department or self-insured employer also has the right to pursue any third party action. *See* RCW 51.24.050.

[279] *Lowry v. City of Auburn*, 2002 Wash. App. 778 (2002) (unpublished).

- Seattle police officer injured by passing motorist while issuing a citation from the side of the roadway;[280]

- Snohomish County deputies assaulted by suspect, when the assault deemed an "independent act of misconduct;"[281]

- Pierce County deputy hit by fellow deputy's vehicle during a foot pursuit;[282] and

- Bellevue officer injured during car accident.[283]

Another issue that arises from time to time is the ability of officers injured in car accidents to collect from uninsured or underinsured motorists. In the past, cities and counties maintained uninsured (UIM) coverage for their employees for such situations. However, AWC and other government insurers dropped this important protection without providing the employees and their union's notice of this significant change (another reminder that AWC works for the interest of the employers, not the employees.) AWC claimed the UIM coverage was unnecessary since the employees were covered by workers compensation, but clearly this is untrue.

Some labor organizations responded to this change by attempting to negotiate for employer-paid replacement coverage, but this effort acquired limited traction. Therefore, injured officers would have to turn to their own policies which may or may not provide such coverage.

---

[280] *Sutton v. Shufelberger*, 31 Wn. App. 579, 643 P.2d 920 (1982).
[281] *Ballou v. Nelson*, 67 Wn. App. 67, 834 P.2d 97 (1992).
[282] *Beaupre v. Pierce County*, 161 Wn.2d 568, 166 P.3d 712 (2007).
[283] *Ward v. Torjussen*, 52 Wn. App. 280, 758 P.2d 1012 (1988).

For example, in *Grange Association v. Jensen*, a King County deputy was found not to have coverage under his uninsured motorist policy for an injury caused by a fleeing suspect because the suspect's intentional actions were not an "accident" within the meaning of the policy.[284] In *Drollinger v. Safeco Ins. Co.*,[285] a Spokane deputy injured from an on-duty accident was denied uninsured motorist coverage simply because he used a pool vehicle rather than having a regularly assigned vehicle. And in *Daley v. Allstate Ins. Co.*,[286] the State Supreme Court held that a Benton County deputy who was injured by an uninsured motorist and had witnessed the death of a State Trooper who was also a personal friend was not able to collect damages for his resulting emotional distress and PTSD. The court held that the UIM policy narrowly covered only physical injuries.

If an injured officer or firefighter recovers damages from a third party wrongdoer, the Department or self-insured employer is legally entitled to a statutory "lien" to reimburse for any worker's compensation benefits paid (again, with the exception of damages for loss of consortium, or emotional distress).[287] The Department and self-insured employer use a spreadsheet to calculate the lien amount, but it is not set in stone and can be negotiated depending on the specific facts at issue in the case.

The best course of action in third party cases is to communicate with the Department or self-insured employer when a settlement or resolution is likely or being considered in order to provide sufficient notice and to determine the specific amount the Department or self-insured employer is seeking to recover as part of the statutory lien. At this point, the injured worker or his or her attorney can negotiate the lien amount with the Department or self-insured employer.

---

[284] 2003 Wash. App. LEXIS 2594 (2003) (unpublished).

[285] 59 Wn. App. 383, 797 P.2d 540 (1990).

[286] 135 Wn.2d 777, 958 P.2d 990 (1998).

[287] RCW 51.24.060(2); *Tobin v. Department of Labor & Industries*, 169 Wn.2d 396, 239 P.3d 544 (2010).

Chapter 10: Conclusion: Some Practical Tips to Navigate the Minefields

In this Chapter we hope to bring everything together for you, giving you a useful summary of what you need to know to help protect your injured or disabled members' rights. This chart may provide a useful and compact visual summary of what forms of legal protections exist. Given the occasional confusion that arises as to what laws relate only to on-duty injuries and what laws apply to all injuries, we identify those distinctions for you:

Legal Protections	On Duty	Off Duty
Disability Discrimination laws (ADA, Rehabilitation Act, WLAD) Accommodation Requirements	X	X
Family Medical Leave Act (FMLA)	X	X
CBA Just Cause protection	X	X
Workers Compensation Time Loss	X	
Industrial Insurance (IIA) Permanent Disability	X	
LEOFF II Supplement	X	
Disability Insurance Policies*	X	X
Social Security Disability	X	X
Public Safety Officers Benefits Act (PSOBA)	X	

*Generally,disability policies do not distinguish the cause of the disability. Occasionally policies have been written to exclude off duty injuries, but most policies extended to public safety employees do not feature this exclusion.

Certainly some protections *by design* are extended only to the officer or firefighter injured on duty. Workers Compensation and its time loss, disability and LEOFF II Supplements are systems designed to compensate an employee hurt at work. Similarly the federal benefits extended under PSOBA are for work related injuries.

Generally, other protections afforded public safety employees do not distinguish based on when or where the injury arose. The requirement to accommodate a disability or provide family leave applies without regard to the cause of the injury. Your contract, absent some special language that you might have for on-duty injuries, is going to extend equal protection to all medical conditions. Disability rights are treated similarly, unless you have a rider that provides a greater level of coverage in the event of an on-duty injury.

There are a number of practical actions you can take as a union representative to improve the situation of your injured members:

Educate Yourself. If you have read through the book so far, you've taken an important step in that direction. Continue to receive updates on the law through newsletters, training and other resources. These laws evolve and court rulings on the FMLA and ADA are dynamic.

Consult Legal Counsel. We designed this book to allow public safety union leaders to be proactive. Much of the information in this book can be put to use without the direct assistance of a lawyer. But some areas are complex and, at times, getting some up-front advice for navigating through these issues can be much better than waiting to place the phone call when the situation is harder to salvage. Some of the issues here are time-sensitive and require a thoughtful response in the moment. A brief phone call can sometimes be the best first step you could take.

Be Proactive with your Troubled Member. If you have an employee with mental health or substance abuse issues, there can be no greater help that you can provide than to get them steered into an assistance program in advance of any employer investigation. The rights to accommodation are recognized far more widely when employees come forward before, rather than after, they are in trouble. If an injury or medical condition limits your member, be sure they are aware in advance of their applicable rights in this process.

Audit your Employer Workers Compensation Practices. Misinformation as to how to calculate the employee compensation in the instance of a workers compensation issue is widespread. Simply put, many Washington public safety employers do it incorrectly. Many do not understand the tax rules surrounding industrial insurance payments or how to coordinate the requirements of the LEOFF II Supplement. Some are not even aware of the LEOFF II Supplement!

Arrange for Cost Effective Disability Coverage. You are going to have members get hurt and some of them are going to lose their careers. You'll need an income protection program in place in the form of disability insurance. Be sure in adopting the program that you understand the tax implications and adopt the program that makes the most sense in light of those tax implications.

Communicate and Cooperate. That's the advice that you'll want to pass forward to your members. While medical confidentiality rules under the ADA limit what information your members must (or should) share, in seeking a disability accommodation, the courts have imposed a clear burden on the employee (and the employer) to share information about potential accommodations. Failure to share that information can cause the loss of the right to an accommodation.

Complete Required FMLA Forms. Similarly, there is a duty on employees to fill out the required forms when seeking Family Leave. There is also an obligation to communicate changing circumstances. On the other hand, as we discussed above, there is no obligation to fill out FMLA paperwork for leave that the employee is not seeking. Under current law, an employer cannot compel FMLA leave just as a way of unloading their FMLA liability.

Insist on FMLA reinstatement. Employers have a right to obtain a second opinion when an employee seeks to return to duty upon return from Family Leave. But they do not have a right to hold up a return to the payroll. The same is true for fitness for duty examinations. While the employer may be able to place the employee on paid administrative leave, they cannot deny pay while they verify information that is solely for their benefit.

Be Fit for Fitness testing. Many bargaining units have negotiated or established contract guidelines that ensure the ADA medical confidentiality rules are adhered to in the Fitness for Duty Examination process. But many have not. Though the parameters of the law are gray, the general view is that the information to which an employer is entitled is restricted and doesn't encompass the entire medical report. Be sure that your procedures do not allow fitness examiners to pass medical secrets onto the boss.

Provide Needed Member Guidance in the Fitness Evaluation Process. During this process, many members are adrift and simply do not understand their rights or what they should do. Unfortunately, many are reluctant, for a variety of reasons, to reach out to union representation when they most need it. They may even unwittingly sign forms that waive their legal and confidentiality protections. The best practice is to address this proactively by educating your members ahead of time.

Practice Your Right to a Second Examination. You and your members are not required to accept as truth the conclusion of the employer's paid examiner. These examination results can and have been successfully challenged. Often you will only be learning of a fitness examination after the member tells you they've been found unfit. At this point, the union should assert itself into the process and determine if a second examination might result in a better finding. The worst thing that happens in such an examination is that you've confirmed for yourself and your member that their options are limited so they can start putting their energies into alternative positions. On the other hand, often these examinations reveal possible accommodations, or even that there is no fitness issue at all.

Brainstorm Regarding Accommodations. Employers are not required to accept any accommodation, but must consider reasonable ones. The required accommodation process is described by courts as a mutual, interactive dialogue. Help your member participate effectively in that dialogue by trying to identify as many potential accommodations as possible.

Make sure you have strong CBA language. If you CBA language says that "discipline" must be for "just cause," get it amended to cover "discharge" as well. Otherwise, you will be allowing the employer a narrower standard of review on any fitness discharge decision. Also make sure that your contract "bill of rights" language contains strong procedural protections.

Remember that Predisicipline rights generally apply. Although PERC has held that there is no *Weingarten* right during the actual fitness interview with the doctor, most of the other predisicipline rights in your CBA or under law apply.

Understand Leave Rights. By far, leave, either paid or unpaid, is the most common form of accommodation of medical conditions. Whether it's reasonable and for how long it's reasonable is context-specific, but courts may allow leaves for up to a year and possibly even longer. You may also have contract terms that specify the procedures and rules around such leaves. Proactive work and discussion with legal counsel go a long way towards understanding your members' rights in this area.

Retain your arbitration rights. Don't agree to "medical arbitration" in the CBA. Employers prefer such language as it truncates your members grounds for challenging a fitness discharge. Doctors, no matter how well-intentioned, are not in the position of judging whether the law requires a particular accommodation. Leave your members rights in the hands of the regular grievance and arbitration process.

Monitor Your Members' on the Job Injury Claims. The L&I Workers compensation system is designed to be user-friendly. Normally, claims can be presented without legal help. But sometimes employers "self-insure" their coverage, which often leads to aggressive tactics that can deny your members their earned benefits. If your members are hitting a roadblock, be sure to at least obtain a consult with a lawyer.

Advise Members of other Disability Payments. As identified above, there are several overlapping forms of disability coverage available. Some depend on whether the injury occurred on duty or off duty. If a permanent disability seems likely, your member should be put in touch with legal counsel.

Remember the Civil Justice Option. While most employees cannot sue their employers for workplace due to the immunity resulting from the workers compensation system this simply is not true for police and firefighters. While there are rules and limits governing such civil claims, if a member is seriously injured, legal counsel should be obtained to review all options. Similarly, your members may have civil litigation rights against third parties.

Prevention is Better than a Cure. The common sense adage is true and applies here. Be proactive on safety issues. Address safety concerns in labor management meetings. Maintain an effective internal safety review process. File complaints when needed to bring the workplace into compliance.

Appendix

PUBLIC SAFETY EMPLOYEES TABLE OF CASES CONCERNING REASONABLE ACCOMMODATIONS

This table lists cases that have examined employee disabilities and determined whether the employee asked for an accommodation, whether the employer granted the accommodation, and whether the accommodation was sufficient to address the disability. It identifies the specific occupation recognizing that different occupations may have different "essential functions" that an employee must qualify to meet. It also lists the relevant statute that protects that disability. The table is divided by type/part of the body and should give you an idea of how similar injuries and disabilities have been treated by employers and the courts.

The law might require different accommodations for different public safety employees based upon their particular occupation. Each occupation has its own set of "essential functions" and to be eligible for an accommodation the employee must meet the minimum essential functions, with or without an accommodation. To help you readily identify and evaluate these cases against a particular situation that you might have, we have **bolded the occupation** at issue in each of these reported cases.

Musculoskeletal
- Neck & Back
- Limbs & Extremities
- Mobility issues
- Other

Vision Disorders

Respiratory Disorders

Circulatory System

Endocrine

Neurological Disorders

Mental & Psychological Disorders

Substance Abuse

MUSCULOSKELETAL

Neck and Back

Disability: Spinal Disability

Accommodation Requested: Transfer to another position

Accommodation Required: No **Accommodation Adequate:** Yes

Citation: *Iverson v. City of Shawnee,* 2008 U.S. Dist. LEXIS 75703 (D. Kan. 2008) **Statute:** ADA

Explanation: After being released for full duty after recovering from a work-related injury, a **Police Officer** was unable to requalify at the firing range. The court held that, though she requested a transfer, because there were no vacant positions her inability to qualify at the firing range disqualified her from police officer duties.

Disability: Spinal Disability; Headaches; Depression

Accommodation Requested: More modifications to courthouse security room

Accommodation Required: Yes **Accommodation Adequate:** Yes

Citation: *Stewart v. County of Brown,* 86 F.3d 107 (7th Cir. 1996) **Statute:** ADA, Rehabilitation Act

Explanation: Deputy Sheriff developed back and neck pain after being assigned to courthouse security TV viewing room. The county provided modifications to lighting, layout, an ergonomic chair, and work schedule that were deemed adequate to accommodate. Though the employee requested further accommodation, court held that the County had fulfilled its duty to provide a reasonable accommodation.

Disability: Spinal Disability: Adhesive Arachnoiditis

Accommodation Requested: Reassignment/light duty

Accommodation Required: Maybe **Accommodation Adequate:** Maybe

Citation: *Patrick v. Henry Cnty.*, 32 AD Cases 59 (N.D. Ga. 2015) **Statute:** ADA

Explanation: After developing adhesive arachnoiditis from treating a patient, a **Firefighter** was denied a light duty position and terminated for his inability to perform the requirements for his full duty position. The County claimed that there were not light duty positions available and if there were, it was not required to offer light duty to him. The Court denied the County's motion for summary judgment because the facts were not clear. The firefighter may proceed with the ADA unlawful discharge and failure-to-accommodate claims.

Disability: Spinal Disability: Congenital Kyphosis; Foot Disability: Hammer Toe

Accommodation Requested: Non-regulation footwear, Removal of gun belt while at desk

Accommodation Required: No

Accommodation Adequate: N/A

Citation: *Lawrence v. Metro-Dade Police Dep't*, 872 F. Supp. 950 (S.D. Fla. 1993)

Statute: Rehabilitation Act

Explanation: Court found that a **Police Sergeant's** conditions did not substantially limit either her ability to work— neither "hammer toes" nor spinal irregularities significantly interfered with the Sargent's patrol duties—or any other aspect of her life. The Sergeant did not make any claim regarding her belt's impact on her *ability* to work at a desk. Note that employer did preemptively accommodate the Sergeant's request for different footwear.

Disability: Spinal Disability: Disk abnormalities, Spinal Stenosis with cord compression

Accommodation Requested: Indefinite extension of light-duty position, transfer to another position

Accommodation Required: No

Accommodation Adequate: N/A

Citation: *Frazier-White v. Gee*, 818 F.3d 1249 (11th Cir. 2016)

Statute: ADA, Florida Civil Rights Act

Explanation: Court found that a **Community Service Officer's** request for an indefinite extension of her light-duty was not a reasonable accommodation because it required the creation of an entirely new position (permanent light-duty. Additionally, the court held that a request for reassignment to an alternative position required the requesting employee to provide the employer with additional information as to what kinds of positions would be acceptable.

Disability: Spinal Disability: Degenerative Disk Disease

Accommodation Requested: Leave of absence

Accommodation Required: No

Accommodation Adequate: N/A

Citation: *Epps v. City of Pine Lawn*, 353 F.3d 588 (8th Cir. 2003)

Statute: ADA

Explanation: City was not required to accommodate a request for a six-month leave of absence from a **Police Officer** with a degenerative disk disease. The court concluded that the officer's excessive absenteeism rendered him unable to perform the essential job function of attendance at work. His accommodation request was not reasonable because the Police Department was small and could not reallocate his duties among staff of 15 to 22 police officers. The City was not required to hire additional officers or assign essential tasks to other employees to make up for his absence.

Disability: Spinal Disability: Degenerative Disk Disease

Accommodation Requested: Reassignment to dispatcher position or other alternative

Accommodation Required: Yes

Accommodation Adequate: Yes

Citation: *Seth v. City of Seattle,* 1999 U.S. App. LEXIS 28046 (9th Cir. 1999)

Statute: ADA

Explanation: A **Police Officer** was forced to retire due to his back problem. He requested accommodations but failed the dispatcher exam. The department sent him letters informing him of available positions, but he was not qualified for other positions. The court held this was adequate accommodation.

Disability: Spinal Disability: Herniated Disk, bulging disk in spine

Accommodation Requested: Reassignment/light duty

Accommodation Required: Yes

Accommodation Adequate: Maybe Not

Citation: *Shapiro v. Twp. of Lakewood,* 292 F.3d 356 (3d Cir. 2002)

Statute: ADA

Explanation: After injuring his back lifting a patient, an **EMT** requested some form of accommodation numerous times. These requests were essentially ignored. Though it is the employee's responsibility to show that there is a vacant position for which they are qualified, the employer is responsible for engaging with the employee to accommodate them. That might mean it is acceptable to circumvent established job application procedures.

Disability: Spinal Disability: Mild Upper Thoracic Scoliosis; Extreme height

Accommodation Requested: Modifications to interior overhead of patrol car, lateral transfer

Accommodation Required: No

Accommodation Adequate: N/A

Citation: *Quinn v. Ohio State Highway Patrol*, No. 2:07-CV-187, 2008 U.S. Dist. LEXIS 73549 (S.D. Ohio Sep. 24, 2008)

Statute: ADA

Explanation: A 6'10" **Trooper Sergeant** requested ADA accommodation for his height when the design of new patrol cars and modifications to the protective cage and overhead shotgun rack provided insufficient room for him to comfortably carry out his duties and resulted in significant back and neck pain. The court found that the sergeant was unable to demonstrate that his condition substantially limited relevant major life activities—sitting, sleeping, lifting, exiting the patrol vehicle/standing up, and working—and thus could not prove a disability under the ADA.

Disability: Spinal Disability: Spina Bifida

Accommodation Requested: To return to previous role (pre-disability) with accommodations

Accommodation Required: Yes

Accommodation Adequate: No

Citation: *McIntyre v. Michigan*, Case No. 1:95-CV-738, 1996 U.S. Dist. LEXIS 19694 (W.D. Mich. Dec. 11, 1996)

Statute: ADA, Mich. Comp. Laws § 37.1101 et seq.

Explanation: Court finds that an employer's restriction of a **Corrections Officer** to light duty in the mail-room was appropriate as accommodation for the employee's limitation, even when the employee's limitation was very specific (a theoretically diminished ability to restrain an inmate).

Disability: Back Disability

Accommodation Requested: Light-duty assignment, transfer

Accommodation Required: Maybe

Accommodation Adequate: No

Citation: *Burch v. City of Nacogdoches*, 174 F.3d 615 (5th Cir. 1999)

Statute: ADA

Explanation: A **Firefighter's** severe back injury disqualified him from continuing work. The court found that, because his injury precluded him from completing even light-duty assignments as a firefighter, and no alternative vacancies were available in the city, his termination for injury was appropriate.

Disability: Back Disability

Accommodation Requested: Exemption from Taser training/Reassignment

Accommodation Required: No

Accommodation Adequate: Yes

Citation: *Robert v. Carter*, 819 F.Supp.2d 832 (S.D. Ind. 2011)

Statute: ADA

Explanation: After a **Civil Deputy Process Server** provided documentation excusing him from Taser training due to back condition, the deputy was given the option to transfer or be terminated. The Court found that the deputy's inability to complete Taser training disqualified him from the job of a merit or civil deputy, and thus his refusal to transfer effectively terminated the interactive process of accommodation.

Disability: Back Disability

Accommodation Requested: Transfer to a position where he did not have to wear gun belt

Accommodation Required: Yes

Accommodation Adequate: No

Citation: *Konewko v. Village of Westchester,* 2000 U.S. Dist. LEXIS 11500 (N.D. Ill. 2000)

Statute: ADA

Explanation: A **Patrol Officer** sued his police department, claiming the department failed to accommodate him by refusing to let him work without a gun belt, which aggravated his back problems. "Though the Court found that apprehending suspects, spending extended periods of time in patrol cars, and wearing a gun belt are essential duties of police officers, the employer failed to seek out the employee after an accommodation request and begin the interactive process of trying to create an accommodation. An employer has an 'affirmative obligation to seek [plaintiff] out and work with [him] to craft a reasonable accommodation, if possible, that would have permitted [his] return to work.'"

Disability: Back Disability

Accommodation Requested: Reinstatement

Accommodation Required: Yes

Accommodation Adequate: Yes

Citation: *Farrell v. Reno,* 983 F. Supp. 1099 (M.D. Fla. 1997)

Statute: ADA

Explanation: As a **US Marshal** healed from a debilitating back injury, he was not entitled to reinstatement until he was fully recovered. Once he recovered, there was no proof that he had been offered jobs that were inferior to the one he held before going on leave. He had turned down the positions he was offered and his employer was not obligated to do more.

Disability: Back Disability

Accommodation Requested: Reassignment

Accommodation Required: Maybe **Accommodation Adequate:** N/A

Citation: *Victor v. State of New Jersey*, 952 A.2d 493 (Unpub. N.J. App. 2008) **Statute:** LAD

Explanation: A **State Trooper** claimed that wearing a protective vest while on road patrol worsened his back injury and he sought reassignment to station duties. The court determined that the trooper's alleged psychological injury resulting from a failure to accommodate his disability was not an adverse personnel action, and damages awarded on the accommodation claim were not segregated from total damages award. The court remanded this case upon conclusion for the disability and race discrimination claims.

Disability: Back Disability

Accommodation Requested: Ability to use cane during shift

Accommodation Required: No **Accommodation Adequate:** N/A

Citation: *Bennett v. State*, 1996 Mich. App. LEXIS 508 (Mich. Ct. App. 1996) **Statute:** Handicappers Civil Rights Act (HCRA); MCL 37.1202(1)(b); MSA 3.550(202)(1)(b)

Explanation: A **Corrections Officer** struggled with back pain, which necessitated his use of a cane. However, despite the use of his cane, he still missed work responsibilities, fell over, and dealt with pain as he climbed stairs because of his condition. His employer would not let him use his cane at work and he sued. The court held that the employer did not fail to accommodate the officer, as even the plaintiff's physician admitted that a cane might prevent some essential functions of his job.

Disability: Back Disability

Accommodation Requested: Limiting assignments to control room/guard tower where plaintiff would have little chance of having to physically confront an inmate

Accommodation Required: No **Accommodation Adequate:** N/A

Citation: *Allison v. Department of* **Statute:** ADA, Rehabilitation Act

Corrections, 94 F.3d 494 (8th Cir. 1996)

Explanation: A **Correctional Officer** hurt her back while on duty, and after taking medical leave was permitted by her doctor to return to work in a limited capacity. However, the department of corrections had a policy of terminating corrections officers who could not perform 100% of the work expected of them. Given the department's knowledge of reasonable accommodations at the time of Allison's termination, which was limited to several instances that were not similar to Allison's, it was reasonable for the department to not accommodate Allisson's disability.

Disability: Back Disability

Accommodation Requested: Continued light duty

Accommodation Required: Yes

Accommodation Adequate: Yes

Citation: *Dancy v. Kline,* 1987 U.S. Dist. LEXIS 2336 (N.D. Ill. 1987)

Statute: Rehabilitation Act

Explanation: A **Federal Protective Officer** had developed disabling pain in his back. He was on light duty for several years and was then terminated. The Court determined that the employer was not required to make the light duty position they had given the employee was permanent, as they were not obligated to create a new position for the employee.

Disability: Back Disability: Permanent

Accommodation Requested: Reassignment

Accommodation Required: Yes

Accommodation Adequate: Yes

Citation: *Pflanz v. City of Cincinnati,* 149 Ohio App.3d 743 (Ohio Ct. App. 2002)

Statute: State Disability Law (R.C. Chapter 4112)

Explanation: A **Firefighter** was terminated for his inability to perform his job after he injured himself trying to catch a woman falling from a stretcher. He claimed he had not been offered any accommodations. The court held that employees have to show that there actually are vacancies in certain positions when they request reassignment to that position. If an equivalent position is not available, offering a lower position is permissible.

Disability: Back Disability: Permanent

Accommodation Requested: Reassignment to light duty

Accommodation Required: Maybe

Accommodation Adequate: N/A

Citation: *Devine v. City of Dallas,* 2000 U.S. Dist. LEXIS 390 (N.D. Tex. 2000)

Statute: ADA

Explanation: A **Firefighter** with an injured back sued when he was terminated for the inability to do his job. He claimed he should have been accommodated by being placed in a dispatcher or an engine company. The firefighter showed enough evidence that he was still capable of performing his duties for the court to deny the city's motion for summary judgement.

Disability: Back Disability: Permanent; Knee Disability: Permanent

Accommodation Requested: Reassignment

Accommodation Required: No

Accommodation Adequate: Yes

Citation: *Johnson v. Otter Tail County,* 2000 U.S. Dist. LEXIS 20671 (D. Minn. 2000)

Statute: ADA

Explanation: The employer was not subject to an interminable duty to reassign employee. The court believed that the **Detention Officer** had been fired before she requested accommodation, but even if she had not been properly terminated prior to her request for accommodation, "the duty to reassign exists for finite period of time, and the outer limits of which the EEOC has limited at no more than six months."

Disability: Back Disability: Temporary

Accommodation Requested: Any (Unclear)

Accommodation Required: No

Accommodation Adequate: N/A

Citation: *Paegle v. DOI,* 813 F. Supp. 61 (D.D.C. 1993)

Statute: Rehabilitation Act

Explanation: A **U.S. Park Police Officer** who was slated to be promoted to sergeant was passed over after injuring his back. Department policy required promotions to be awarded only to those capable of fulfilling the duties of the role, and the officer could not do so with his injury. Court held that because the injury was temporary and the officer's opportunity for promotion would be there following his recovery (in fact, the officer was promoted once he was asymptomatic for six months), it did not qualify as a "disability" under the Rehabilitation Act and he could not expect reasonable accommodation.

Disability: Back Disability: Lower-back

Accommodation Requested: Continued payment of salary

Accommodation Required: Yes

Accommodation Adequate: N/A

Citation: *Conomikes v. Libous*, 63 A.D.2d 1109, 406 N.Y.S.2d 397 (App. Div. 1978)

Statute: N.Y. CLS Gen. Mun. § 207-a

Explanation: Court determined that a **Fire Training Instructor's** position was too strenuous to be classified as light-duty work. The instructor's lower-back injury therefore disqualified him from the position, and the employer was prevented from terminating his employment.

Disability: Back Disability; Knee Disability

Accommodation Requested: Reassignment

Accommodation Required: Yes

Accommodation Adequate: Yes

Citation: *Dedman v. Wash. Personnel Appeals Bd.*, 98 Wn.App. 471 (Wash. Ct. App. 1999)

Statute: WLAD

Explanation: Washington State DOC was not required to accommodate disabled **Corrections Officer** by permanently assigning her to a control booth position. Her requested accommodation was to be assigned to a position that did not involve any inmate contact. The court concluded that the ability to restrain an inmate was an essential function of a corrections officer job and, that by virtue of her disabilities; she was unable to perform essential duties. Permanent assignments to otherwise rotating/temporary positions restrict the employer's flexibility and create a hardship.

Disability: Back Disability, Neck Disability, Shoulder Disability, Leg Disability

Accommodation Requested: Reassignment

Accommodation Required: Yes

Accommodation Adequate: Yes

Citation: *Keever v. City of Middletown*, 145 F.3d 809 (6th Cir. 1998)

Statute: ADA

Explanation: City's accommodation of **Police Officer's** work-related injury was found reasonable where it offered him a desk job, even though it was not his preferred accommodation—a transfer to night shift. An employer has discretion to choose which reasonable accommodation it will provide. The offer to transfer to a desk job with reduced physical and mental responsibilities, in combination with allowing him to take leave as necessary, the court holds, was reasonable given his disability.

Disability: Back Disability, Knee Disability

Accommodation Requested: Reinstatement

Accommodation Required: No

Accommodation Adequate: N/A

Citation: *Briscoe v. Vill. of Vernon Hills*, No. 15 C 10761, 2016 U.S. Dist. LEXIS 68459 (N.D. Ill. May 25, 2016)

Statute: ADA

Explanation: Former **Police Commander** with back and knee injuries refused to return to work and violated department policy by engaging in secondary employment. After being disciplined for the violation, the Commander resigned. Court determined that the commander was not fit to perform the duties of his position, and thus was not afforded a right of reasonable accommodation under the ADA.

Disability: Neck Disability; Back Disability

Accommodation Requested: Reassignment

Accommodation Required: Yes

Accommodation Adequate: No

Citation: *Cripe v. City of San Jose*, 261 F.3d 877 (9th Cir. 2001)

Statute: ADA

Explanation: The court holds a city policy—that **Police Officers** whose disabilities prevented them from fulfilling a beat-patrol requirement could not receive specialized assignments and were only eligible for non-patrol positions—did not call for reasonable accommodations and, therefore, violated the ADA. Even though the seniority system in the officer union's CBA was applicable, the City's argument that varying contract terms might generate resentment among officers and undermine morale did not constitute an "undue hardship" analysis nor provide a basis for a "business necessity" defense.

Disability: Neck Disability; Back Disability

Accommodation Requested: Promotion

Accommodation Required: Maybe

Accommodation Adequate: N/A

Citation: *Roberts v. City of Dallas*, 1999 U.S. Dist. LEXIS 2052 (N.D. Tex. 1999)

Statute: ADA

Explanation: A **Police Officer** was injured during a riot and placed on desk duty. She applied for a promotion which would have permitted her to continue her work but earn more money. She ranked 3rd of the 600 who took the promotion exam. The department then declared the ability to perform street patrol a prerequisite to the position the officer applied for. She did not receive the promotion. The court held that there was a material question of fact as to whether or not the ability to do street patrol was an essential function of the position that the officer had applied for. She was permitted to continue her case and summary judgment in favor of the defendants was denied.

Disability: Neck Disability: Constant Neck Pain, Decreased Mobility in Left Arm

Accommodation Requested: Transfer to computer task force

Accommodation Required: Maybe

Accommodation Adequate: N/A

Citation: *Breitfelder v. Leis,* 151 Fed. Appx. 379 (6th Cir. 2005)

Statute: ADA; Rehabilitation Act

Explanation: After being injured at work, a **Detective** experienced ongoing problems with extreme pain. He requested to be transferred to the division investigating computer crime, but this request was denied. The detective could not perform work in even a sedentary position, and was therefore disqualified.

Limbs and Extremities

Disability: Arm Disability: Limited mobility in left arm and hand, no grip strength

Accommodation Requested: Reassignment to administrative correctional lieutenant peace officer job

Accommodation Required: No

Accommodation Adequate: N/A

Citation: *Furtado v. State Personnel Board*, Cal. App. Lexis 8 (2013)

Statute: ADA

Explanation: After a **Correctional Lieutenant** working at a state prison had an auto accident, injuries to his left arm and hand caused him to lack the range of motion and sufficient grip strength to use a baton in his left hand. He was denied a requested reassignment to an administrative correctional lieutenant peace officer job. The court concluded that, even while performing administrative duties, a correctional lieutenant had to be able to subdue an aggressive prisoner and use a baton.

Disability: Arm Disability: Completely disabled upper left arm

Accommodation Requested: Permanent light duty

Accommodation Required: No

Accommodation Adequate: Yes

Citation: *Champ v. Baltimore County,* 884 F. Supp. 991 (D. Md. 1995)

Statute: ADA; Rehabilitation Act

Explanation: After a **Police Officer** was injured in an off-duty motorcycle accident he lost complete use of his upper left arm. He was supposed to be permitted only 251 days of light duty but was given 16 years of light duty. When he was terminated after budget problems because he couldn't perform all of the essential functions of a police officer he held that the department had not accommodated him and that he could still fire a gun and drive an emergency vehicle. The court found that he still could not meet the requirement of being able to perform a forcible arrest and the employee provided no possible accommodation that could help him perform this function.

Disability: Arm Disability: Restricted use of right arm due to blood vessel tumors

Accommodation Requested: Examination

Accommodation Required: Yes **Accommodation Adequate:** Yes

Citation: *Ethridge v. State of Alabama,* 860 F. Supp. 808 (M.D. Ala. 1994) **Statute:** ADA

Explanation: **Police Officer Applicant** with limited use of his right arm failed handgun retest at the police academy, and could not successfully complete handgun course required under state law. The court held that the State provided an acceptable and reasonable accommodation by permitting him to shoot with one hand instead of two. The handgun course curriculum was established by standards and training commission created by state law, and the court determined that a handgun qualification course was necessary to ensure the safety of police officers and the community.

Disability: Arm Disability: Myositis of right arm, epicondylitis of right elbow and hand; Foot Disability: thrombophlebitis lower left foot, varicose veins; Myasthenia

Accommodation Requested: Light duty

Accommodation Required: No **Accommodation Adequate:** N/A

Citation: *Blissitt v. Chicago,* 1990 U.S. Dist. LEXIS 5132 (N.D. Ill. 1990) **Statute:** Rehabilitation Act

Explanation: An officer began experiencing debilitating pain and weakness in her right arm, preventing her from being able to fulfill her duties as a **Police Officer**. She was placed on medical leave. After healing she requested reinstatement in a light duty assignment but was denied. The court held that this was appropriate. Light duty assignments were for those who had been injured on duty, which the plaintiff was not. They had accommodated her through medical leave.

Disability: Arm Disability: Occasional, unpredictable numbness in left arm; Headaches

Accommodation Requested: Reinstatement or transfer to a position comparable to that of her former position

Accommodation Required: No

Accommodation Adequate: Yes

Citation: *Blumhagen v. Clackamas County*, 91 Ore. App. 510 (Or. Ct. App. 1988)

Statute: Or. Rev. Stat. §§ 659.415, 659.420, and 659.425

Explanation: A **Police Officer** was in a car and was given light duty for nine months but was ultimately terminated, after which she accepted a position with a different employer that provided less compensation than her position as a police officer. Afterwards, the department created several new positions closer in status to her old job, but did not hire the employee. The court held that the department had not failed to accommodate the officer, because they had provided accommodation through medical leave and she had removed herself from special consideration after accepting a new job.

Disability: Hand Disability: Missing fingers

Accommodation Requested: None

Accommodation Required: No

Accommodation Adequate: N/A

Citation: *Stratton v. Mo. Dep't of Corrs. & Human Res.*, 897 S.W.2d 1 (Mo. Ct. App. 1995)

Statute: ADA

Explanation: A **Police Officer Candidate** missing four fingers on one hand was considered unqualified for the position because he could not perform the essential functions of the job "with or without accommodation," even though he had previously worked for the employer in the same role.

Disability: Hand Disability: Stunted left hand

Accommodation Requested: Placement in a position commensurate with completion of officer training

Accommodation Required: No

Accommodation Adequate: N/A

Citation: *Mathes v. Harris Cty.*, No. 00-20651, 2002 U.S. App. LEXIS 28943 (5th Cir. Jan. 17, 2002)

Statute: ADA

Explanation: Court held that a **Sherriff's Academy Cadet's** claim of disability discrimination against the Sherriff's academy for dismissal was unsubstantiated. The cadet's claim effectively constituted a claim of failure to promote, but the he conceded that he could not be a fully functioning officer due to his disability, so he would not have qualified for the position of officer regardless.

Disability: Hand Disability: No left hand

Accommodation Requested: Individual assessment of capability to meet licensing requirements

Accommodation Required: Yes

Accommodation Adequate: N/A

Citation: *Stillwell v. Kan. City Bd. of Police Comm'rs*, 872 F. Supp. 682 (W.D. Mo. 1995)

Statute: ADA

Explanation: After legislation passed requiring all armed security guards to meet the physical requirements and qualifications of city police officers in order to be licensed, a **Private Security Guard** was not allowed to renew his license due to his lack of a left hand. The court found that the loss of a hand qualifies as a "disability" under the ADA, that a blanket ban on individuals suffering from a disability was a violation of the Act, and that all future licensing had to be based on individual assessments of applicants.

Disability: Hand Disability

Accommodation Requested: Reinstatement and permanent assignment to control center

Accommodation Required: Yes

Accommodation Adequate: No

Citation: *Anglin v. Department of Corrections*, 160 Ore. App. 463 (Or. Ct. App. 1999)

Statute: Or. Rev. Stat. § 659.410 et seq.

Explanation: A **Corrections Officer** fractured his hand, resulting in permanent pain and damage to his hand. He was deemed unable to perform essential functions of his job and terminated, despite his request to be accommodated by a permanent assignment to the control room. The court determined that a control room assignment was a viable accommodation, holding that the employer could not hold an entire job classification or profession off-limits. As long as he could be accommodated in the control room and perform one corrections officer position, he should not have been terminated.

Disability: Hand Disability: Use of only one hand

Accommodation Requested: Modified equipment

Accommodation Required: Maybe

Accommodation Adequate: N/A

Citation: *Taylor v. Hampton Rds. Reg'l Jail Auth.*, 550 F. Supp. 2d 614 (E.D.

Statute: ADA, Rehabilitation Act

Va. 2008)

Explanation: Court held that an employer's vague and conclusory objections were insufficient to counter a **Corrections Officer's** evidence that she could accomplish all the necessary functions of the position with reasonable accommodation. Additionally, an employee's self-assessment of their disabled status has no bearing on their classification as "disabled" under the ADA; "a plaintiff's 'optimistic self-assessment [regarding their abilities]… deserves little weight.'"

Disability: Hand Disability: Carpal Tunnel Syndrome

Accommodation Requested: Ergonomically correct desk and keyboard, as well as an assistant to help her with typing

Accommodation Required: Maybe **Accommodation Adequate:** N/A

Citation: *Frazier v. Smith,* 12 F. Supp. 2d 1362 (S.D. Ga. 1998) **Statute:** ADA

Explanation: A **Jail Administrator** requested accommodation and the request was denied. The court held that there was enough evidence of failure to accommodate to permit the question to go to trial.

Disability: Hand Disability: Wrist injury

Accommodation Requested: Reinstatement and permission to wear brace

Accommodation Required: No **Accommodation Adequate:** N/A

Citation: *Yodice v. Metropolitan Dade County,* 1995 U.S. Dist. LEXIS 21872 (S.D. Fla. 1995) **Statute:** ADA

Explanation: The employee **Police Officer** "suggests that she is able to perform the essential functions of a police officer if she is allowed the reasonable accommodation of wearing a brace." However, the employer already permitted this accommodation. The employee still suffered from hypersensitivity in her wrist, placing herself and others at risk of losing control of her hand if she were hit in that area.

Disability: Hand Disability: Hand tremors

Accommodation Requested: Reinstatement

Accommodation Required: Yes **Accommodation Adequate:** Yes

Citation: *Fussell v. Georgia Ports Auth.,* 906 F. Supp. 1561 (S.D. Ga. 1995) **Statute:** ADA

Explanation: The employer was not required to permit a **Police Officer** to stay employed in that position when he continually failed a firearm qualification test." He presented too great of a danger to others because it was not clear that he could shoot straight. The employer was also not required to stay in contact with the employee and inform him when other positions opened up. It is the employee's responsibility to stay in touch and if he cannot be bothered to do so the employer does not need to continually seek the employee out after termination.

Disability: Shoulder Disability

Accommodation Requested: Reinstatement, consideration for promotion

Accommodation Required: Yes

Accommodation Adequate: Yes

Citation: *Kincaid v. City of Omaha,* 378 F.3d 799 (8th Cir. 2004)

Statute: ADA

Explanation: An employer required a **Correctional Officer** to provide medical release from their doctor before accommodating the employee. The court held this was reasonable.

Disability: Shoulder Disability: Previously Separated Shoulder

Accommodation Requested: Renewed Consideration of Job Application

Accommodation Required: No

Accommodation Adequate: N/A

Citation: *Curcio v. Nassau Cty. Civil Serv. Comm'n*, 220 A.D.2d 412, 631 N.Y.S.2d 881 (App. Div. 1995)

Statute: N.Y. Exec Law § 292(1)(a)

Explanation: Court found that denying a **Police Officer Applicant** due to a previously separated should was not a violation of the ADA. A previously separated should does not qualify as a "disability" under the ADA, and the risk of further injury and incapacitation associated with the condition was significant enough to bear weight in the decision to not employ a police officer.

Disability: Charcot-Marie-Tooth Disease; Hand tremors

Accommodation Requested: Limited to assignments not requiring firearm proficiency

Accommodation Required: No

Accommodation Adequate: N/A

Citation: *Johnson v. Maryland,* 940 F. Supp. 873 (D. Md. 1996)

Statute: ADA

Explanation: A **Corrections Officer** suffered from hand tremors which impacted his ability to be firearm certified. He requested that he only be assigned to positions that didn't require firearm proficiency, but the court held that this was an unreasonable accommodation.

Mobility Issues

Disability: Foot Disability: Injured heel

Accommodation Requested: Permanent light duty

Accommodation Required: No

Accommodation Adequate: N/A

Citation: *Feeley v. New York City Police Dep't,* 2001 U.S. Dist. LEXIS 25431 (E.D.N.Y. 2001)

Statute: ADA

Explanation: **Transit Police Officer** injured her heel, took two months of leave, and returned to work in a light duty capacity. She was eventually cleared for full duty but was terminated when she failed to report. She claimed she should have been permanently placed on light duty. The court held that the position was only intended to be temporary, and the employer did not have to create a new permanent position to accommodate the officer. Furthermore, the officer admitted that she was not capable of performing the essential functions of her job, so the employer was permitted to terminate her.

Disability: Foot Disability: Ankle Fracture

Accommodation Requested: Policy, transfer

Accommodation Required: Yes

Accommodation Adequate: Yes

Citation: *Molloy v. City of Bellevue*, 71 Wash.App. 382 (Wash. Ct. App. 1993)

Statute: WLAD

Explanation: The City of Bellevue's offer of dispatcher position to a former **Police Officer** with permanent partial disability in his left ankle was a reasonable accommodation, even though the dispatcher position only paid half his previous patrol officer salary. The police department had a policy that all officers must be able to perform all duties of a police officer in order to adequately protect the public, and the officer conceded that he could no longer carry out the essential functions of a patrol position. The City had no duty to exempt him from this policy or to create a special position for him within the Police Department.

Disability: Foot Disability: Nerve damage

Accommodation Requested: Disability Allowance

Accommodation Required: No

Accommodation Adequate: N/A

Citation: *Bd. of Trs. of the Okla. City Police Pension & Ret. Sys. v. Clark*, 1983 OK 4, 661 P.2d 506

Statute: Okla. Stat. tit. 11, §§ 50-101 et. Seq. (1977)

Explanation: A **Patrolman** injured in the line of duty was reassigned to the communications unit and, when he was unable to return to active duty, filed for disability allowance. Court found that where an officer is permanently and limitedly disabled, as long as he is capable of satisfactorily performing alternative duties he is not unfit for duty and thus not entitled to disability allowance.

Disability: Foot Disability: Injured ankle, limits on running, walking, standing, etc.

Accommodation Requested: Assignment to dispatched position at pay rate of police officer

Accommodation Required: No

Accommodation Adequate: N/A

Citation: *Conklin v. City of Englewood,* 98 F.3d 1341 (6th Cir. 1996)

Statute: ADA

Explanation: The court held that a **Police Officer** was not disabled, but even if he were considered disabled the department had not failed to accommodate him. It was not a reasonable accommodation to request that essential functions of the police officer position were transferred to others because the employee could not do them with his injured ankle. Furthermore, requesting reinstatement as a dispatcher at the pay rate of a police officer essentially would have required the employer to create a new position, which they were not obligated to do.

Disability: Hip Disability: Femoral hip impingement, torn labrum

Accommodation Requested: Assign to another vehicle with more leg room

Accommodation Required: No

Accommodation Adequate: N/A

Citation: *Koty v. Zaruba*, 2015 AD Cases 186829 (N.D. Ill. 2015)

Statute: ADA

Explanation: **Police Officer's** inability to drive a smaller patrol car due to hip pain was not a protected disability.

Disability: Hip Disability: Artificial hip

Accommodation Requested: Restructuring job, relieve him of responsibility to be able to restrain inmates

Accommodation Required: Maybe

Accommodation Adequate: N/A

Citation: *Wilson v. County of*

Statute: ADA

Bernalillo, 2000 U.S. App. LEXIS 7752 (10th Cir. 2000)

Explanation: Restraining inmates is an essential duty for a **Corrections Officer** and an employee cannot be relieved of this responsibility. Not only is it unreasonable under the ADA, but it also places the employee's coworkers in danger.

Disability: Knee Disability: Permanent

Accommodation Requested: Reinstatement

Accommodation Required: Yes

Accommodation Adequate: Yes

Citation: *Perdick v. City of Allentown,* 2014 U.S. Dist. LEXIS 24980 (E.D. Pa. 2014)

Statute: ADA

Explanation: After a **Police Officer** returned from leave resulting from his knee injury, he was placed in the records department. He knew officers received light duty upon their return, but that it was only for six months. He was offered a number of positions outside the police department since he was technically an employee of the city and not just the department. He turned them all down, and when his light duty ran out he was terminated. The court upheld his termination, stating that the employer had initiated the accommodation process but the officer had brought that process to a close by failing to respond to any of the job offers he was given.

Disability: Knee Disability

Accommodation Requested: Permanent light-duty assignment, reassignment

Accommodation Required: No

Accommodation Adequate: N/A

Citation: *Raiford v. Md. Dep't of Juvenile Servs.*, 31 AD Cases 1464 (D. Md. 2015)

Statute: ADA

Explanation: A **Resident Advisor Trainee** at a juvenile detention facility did not have a valid claim for failure to accommodate under the ADA after suffering a knee injury on the job. He was unable to perform essential job functions, including physical restraint and detainee supervision, his request to be placed on light duty permanently was unreasonable, and there was not a vacant position performing different duties.

Disability: Knee Disability

Accommodation Requested: Light-duty assignment or paid leave

Accommodation Required: No

Accommodation Adequate: N/A

Citation: *Matter of Abram v. N.Y. State Div. of Human Rights*, 2010 NY Slip Op 2279, 71 A.D.3d 1471, 896 N.Y.S.2d 764 (App. Div.)

Statute: ADA

Explanation: A **Police Officer** who suffered a knee injury at work failed to show that any light-duty positions were available—in other words, that the requested accommodation was reasonable—or that paid leave was otherwise reasonable.

Disability: Knee Disability; Hand Disability

Accommodation Requested: Parking space

Accommodation Required: Yes

Accommodation Adequate: Maybe

Citation: *Price v. City of New York*, 797 F. Supp. 2d 219 (E.D.N.Y. 2011)

Statute: ADA

Explanation: City **Corrections Officer** with injuries to both knees and right hand could proceed to trial with a failure-to accommodate claim based on the City's denial of his request for a handicapped parking space. Eventually the City provided him a space, but he then alleged that space provided was insufficient because it was too far away and would require standing at a bus stop. The court found that a triable question arose as to whether the City's offer was reasonable and it allowed to the officer to proceed to trial on his request for a better parking spot.

Disability: Leg Disability: Amputated leg

Accommodation Requested: Reassignment

Accommodation Required: Yes

Accommodation Adequate: Yes

Citation: *Rehling v. City of Chicago*, 207 F.3d 1009 (7th Cir. 2000)

Statute: ADA

Explanation: Though a **Police Officer** wanted to work in the district where he had been assigned before he lost his leg, the department had provided reasonable accommodation by offering two other positions. "It is well-established that an employer is obligated to provide a qualified individual with a reasonable accommodation, not the accommodation he would prefer."

Disability: Polio

Accommodation Requested: Motorized transportation from her car to her office and for use throughout the work spaces, railing and chairs to help her get around

Accommodation Required: Maybe

Accommodation Adequate: N/A

Citation: *Bagatti v. Department of Rehabilitation*, 97 Cal. App. 4th 344 (Cal. App. 3d Dist. 2002)

Statute: Fair Housing and Employment Act (California state law)

Explanation: A **Corrections Clerk** struggled to walk long distances while at her job, which required her to traverse long distances within the facility. She requested an accommodation involving motorized transportation or the placement of handrails and chairs throughout the building to help her move around. The court held she had a viable claim and permitted her to move forward with her case, contrary to the holding of the lower court.

Disability: Quadriplegia

Accommodation Requested: Waiver of weapons-firing and forceful arrest duties

Accommodation Required: No

Accommodation Adequate: N/A

Citation: *Coski v. Denver*, 795 P.2d 1364 (Colo. App. 1990)

Statute: Colo. Rev. Stat. § 24-34-402

Explanation: Court found that the necessary worksite modifications required to accommodate a paraplegic **Corrections Officer** created too great a financial burden to be reasonable, and that a job-restructuring would have created costly inefficiencies in the distribution of job duties. The court held that a firing a weapon and making a forceful arrest were essential job functions because it was reasonable to require all officers to engage in those activities.

Disability: Paraplegia

Accommodation Requested: Reassignment

Accommodation Required: Yes

Accommodation Adequate: No

Citation: *Stone v. City Of Mount Vernon*, 118 F.3d 92 (2nd Cir. 1997)

Statute: ADA

Explanation: Paraplegic former **Firefighter** was found by the court to have presented sufficient evidence to demonstrate that his permanent assignment to fire department's fire alarm bureau or fire prevention bureau would be a reasonable accommodation. Despite the employer's claims that the position required certain skills that the employee no longer had, there was no history of those skills being called on. The court explained that each reasonable accommodation request must be decided on the basis of then existing circumstances, and recognized that the number of incumbent employees with disabilities could be a material factor to be considered to the extent that an employer needed to hire a certain number of persons without a disability. The court concluded that hiring 5-10 disabled persons would be an undue hardship is not a credible defense when an employer had hired none.

Disability: Paraplegia

Accommodation Requested: Permanent administrative position

Accommodation Required: No

Accommodation Adequate: N/A

Citation: *Ensslin v. Twp. of N. Bergen*, 275 N.J. Super. 352, 646 A.2d 452 (Super. Ct. App. Div. 1994)

Statute: N.J. Stat. Ann. § 10:5-29.1

Explanation: Court held that a paraplegic **Police Officer's** inability to perform functions central to the responsibilities of a police officer precluded him from the accommodation of a permanent administrative role, because even such administrative positions required an ability to watch, apprehend, and secure suspect and prisoners.

Disability: Paraplegia

Accommodation Requested: Reinstatement

Accommodation Required: No

Accommodation Adequate: N/A

Citation: *Simon v. St. Louis County*, 735 F.2d 1082 (8th Cir. 1984)

Statute: Rehabilitation Act

Explanation: Even though the **Police Officer** could perform four of the positions that officers were expected to rotate through, the department's refusal to reinstate him in only those positions was not unreasonable. He could not perform two of the essential functions of a police officer—forceful arrest and transfer to all positions in the department.

Disability: Sacroiliac Joint Dysfunction

Accommodation Requested: Reinstatement with sick leave

Accommodation Required: No

Accommodation Adequate: N/A

Citation: *Robert v. Board of County Commissioners of Brown County*, U.S. App. Lexis 18365 (10th Cir. 2012)

Statute: ADA, FMLA

Explanation: After a **County Adult Intensive Supervision Officer** developed sacroiliac joint dysfunction, rendering her unable to work outside of her home or to visit the offenders in the jail or at their homes, she was granted a lengthy leave of absence. When she was still unable to perform all of her job functions after her leave, she was fired. The court rejected both claims as she could not show that she could return to her job, with or without reasonable accommodations, when her FMLA leave ended: she was not an "otherwise qualified" disabled person, and at the time she was fired, the employer had no reasonable estimate of when, if ever, she would be able to resume all of her essential job functions.

Other

Disability: Arthritis: Rheumatoid

Accommodation Requested: Not Stated

Accommodation Required: No

Accommodation Adequate: N/A

Citation: *Kaplan v. City of N. Las Vegas*, 323 F.3d 1226 (9th Cir. 2003)

Statute: ADA

Explanation: A **Deputy Marshal** injured his hand during training and during treatment was also diagnosed with rheumatoid arthritis in his arm. Unable to effectively perform duties essential to his position, he was terminated with reference to his permanent rheumatoid arthritis even though his limitations were due to the work injury, from which he recovered in time. The Court held that the deputy marshal could not bring an ADA claim because though his employer misattributed his inability to perform essential duties to his rheumatoid arthritis, which *would* qualify as a disability if it were the cause of his limitations, the deputy marshal was not actually disabled by the arthritis and thus not disabled under the ADA.

Disability: Arthritis; Hip replacement

Accommodation Requested: Alternative method to reach basement dispatcher office such as elevator repair

Accommodation Required: Yes

Accommodation Adequate: No

Citation: *Littlefield v. York County,* 2000 U.S. Dist. LEXIS 20907, 2000 WL 760959 (D. Me. 2000)

Statute: ADA

Explanation: A **Dispatcher** with arthritis requested an accommodation in order to help her go up and down the stairs to the dispatcher office. A chairlift was eventually installed, but in order for an accommodation to be reasonable, it must be timely. The employer installed chair lift to assist with ascending and descending stairs eleven months after employee resigned because of lack of accommodation. The employer was required to look into other methods of accommodating the employee other than the method the dispatcher initially suggested in order to provide a timely accommodation.

Disability: Arthritis: Rheumatoid; injury that exacerbated this condition

Accommodation Requested: Retraining, reinstatement in a different position

Accommodation Required: Maybe **Accommodation Adequate:** N/A

Citation: *Warren v. Volusia County*, 188 Fed. Appx. 859 (11th Cir. 2006) **Statute:** ADA

Explanation: The burden to request an accommodation is on the employee. While the **Corrections Officer** was not privileged to reasonable accommodation because they did not request the accommodation. Information provided to the employer by the doctor does not count as a request for accommodation, as the doctor was not functioning as her representative. Additionally, retraining was not considered a reasonable accommodation by the court.

Disability: Degenerative Joint Disease

Accommodation Requested: Permanent light duty position

Accommodation Required: No **Accommodation Adequate:** Yes

Citation: *Gera v. County of Schuylkill*, 2015 AD Cases 186185 (3d Cir. 2015) **Statute:** ADA

Explanation: Due to the former **Correctional Officer's** mobility impairment, he maintained a light duty position for three years until he was discharged. He filed disability and retaliation claims against the county but they were dismissed. The Court determined that where he is unable to perform essential duties of inmate control, the officer failed to identify a vacant position for which he was qualified. Additionally. an almost three-year gap between his requested accommodation and discharge, standing alone, was not sufficient to raise inference of retaliation.

Disability: Degenerative Joint Disease

Accommodation Requested: Transfer to computer data entry position

Accommodation Required: No **Accommodation Adequate:** N/A

Citation: *Hastings v. Department of Corrections*, 110 Cal. App. 4th 963 (Cal. App. 3d Dist. 2003) **Statute:** California Fair Employment and Housing Act (FEHA)

Explanation: During a period of conditional employment during which a **Correctional Peace Officer Cadet** was completing Basic Correctional Officer Academy, the cadet injured his knees. Doctors discovered a permanent joint disease in his knees, and his ability to walk and stand became very limited. He required a cane to walk more than a few steps and could not stand for long. The court held that the employer was not required to accommodate the cadet because he was completely unable to perform the job duties he would need as a correctional officer.

Disability: Degenerative Joint Disease

Accommodation Requested: Permanent assignment to tower duty

Accommodation Required: No

Accommodation Adequate: N/A

Citation: *Martin v. Kansas,* 996 F. Supp. 1282 (D. Kan. 1998)

Statute: ADA

Explanation: A **Corrections Officer** with mobility issues wanted to be permanently assigned to tower duty, which accommodated his needs. However, this would have constituted permanent light duty, which was not deemed a reasonable accommodation.

Disability: Degenerative joint disease: Ehlers Danlos Syndrome

Accommodation Requested: Electric door; work from home; parking lot maintenance

Accommodation Required: Yes

Accommodation Adequate: No

Citation: *Sturz v. Wisconsin Dept. of Corrections*, 642 F. Supp. 2d 881 (2009)

Statute: Rehabilitation Act

Explanation: Federal court allowed a **Former Parole Officer** with a degenerative joint condition to proceed with a constructive discharge claim arising under the Rehabilitation Act, where there was evidence that a failure to accommodate her disability exacerbated her impairment. Court did hold that the general policy prohibiting employees from working from home was not inherently unreasonable.

Disability: Degenerative Joint Disease

Accommodation Requested: Allow him to remain in DARE program or similar position

Accommodation Required: Maybe

Accommodation Adequate: N/A

Citation: *Dorris v. City of Kentwood,* 1994 U.S. Dist. LEXIS 15640 (W.D. Mich. 1994)

Statute: ADA

Explanation: Because it was unclear whether or not the ability to perform patrol duties was an essential function of the **Police Officer's** job, the court permitted the plaintiff officer to continue with his suit. He had been a DARE officer and had never performed any duties associated with patrol, but when he requested to be permanently assigned to the DARE position, his employer insisted that he needed to be able to perform at a patrol level.

Disability: Inflammatory muscle disease (inclusion body myositis)

Accommodation Requested: Reassignment

Accommodation Required: Yes

Accommodation Adequate: Maybe

Citation: *Reilly v. Upper Darby Township*, 809 F. Supp. 2d 368 (E.D. Penn. 2011)

Statute: ADA

Explanation: A township **Police Officer** fired after developing an inflammatory muscle disease could proceed to trial with his failure-to-accommodate claim. He claimed that his denial of a reassignment to non-patrol job violated the ADA. The township argued that his assignment to permanent control-room job would have posed an "undue hardship." It cited the limited budget for officers and the fact that lower-paid civilians staff those jobs. The court ruled that the officer could proceed to trial to determine the reasonableness of his proposed accommodations: 1) that active-duty officers already staffed the control room on the night shift; 2) that he would accept night shift position; and 3) that he would move, if necessary, to meet the township's residency requirement in order to qualify for civilian control-room positions.

Disability: Shattered Pelvis

Accommodation Requested: Reinstatement, part-time shifts

Accommodation Required: Maybe

Accommodation Adequate: No

Citation: *Kelley v. Corr. Med. Servs., Inc.*, 2013 U.S. App. Lexis 2588 (1st Cir.)

Statute: ADA

Explanation: A **Correctional Medical Nurse** who suffered an off-duty injury needed surgery and had a number of restrictions, including using crutches and not using her hands for lifting. Her ability to bend and squat was also limited. The court found that the nurse presented sufficient evidence where a jury could conclude that her supervisor was hostile to any accommodation of her disability, based on both comments and actions. The jury could have concluded that the nurse's refusal to obey one instruction from that supervisor was only a "convenient pretext" for firing an employee who had repeatedly asked for accommodations of her disability.

VISION DISORDERS

Disability: Blepharospas; Tardive dystonia; Psychiatric issues

Accommodation Requested: Relief from obligation to perform courtroom coverage in specific courtrooms

Accommodation Required: Maybe

Accommodation Adequate: N/A

Citation: *Kriegel v. Rhode Island*, 266 F. Supp. 2d 288 (D.R.I. 2003)

Statute: Rhode Island Fair Employment Practices Act ("FEPA"), Rhode Island Civil Rights of Individuals with Handicaps Act ("RICRIHA"), Rhode Island Civil Rights Act ("RICRA")

Explanation: A **Probation and Parole Counselor** requested removal from the obligation to cover specific courtrooms that required rapid eye scanning. His visual problems made doing so difficult. After he requested the accommodation he was informed that his request had been denied. He appealed the request, but was simply told that monitoring the two courtrooms were an essential function of his job. The court concluded that there had been no attempt by the employer to accommodate the counselor, and he was permitted to continue with his failure to accommodate claim.

Disability: Blindness

Accommodation Requested: Braille computer

Accommodation Required: Yes

Accommodation Adequate: Yes

Citation: *Leine v. California Dep't of Rehabilitation*, 1999 U.S. App. LEXIS 32521 (9th Cir. 1999)

Statute: ADA, Rehabilitation Act

Explanation: Though the employer took 19 months to provide the **Corrections Employee** with a Braille computer, employers are not required to provide employees with the accommodation they prefer, only reasonable accommodations. Throughout the wait for a Braille computer the employer provided a reader, driver, and other assistants to help the corrections employee perform her job. The employer also brought in a specialist who ultimately provided a better computer than the one the employee requested.

Disability: Blindness in one eye, partial vision in other eye

Accommodation Requested: Assistance in performing some duties, only receiving specific types of cases

Accommodation Required: No

Accommodation Adequate: N/A

Citation: *Holbrook v. City of Alpharetta,* 112 F.3d 1522 (11th Cir. 1997)

Statute: ADA; Rehabilitation Act

Explanation: A **Detective** with poor vision had been provided with accommodations, but when they were ceased he claimed that the department was obligated to continue them. The court held that the department did not have to continue providing the accommodations, as they were unreasonable. He had received specific case assignments and assistance collecting certain types of evidence, but this was beyond what the department needed to do and the detective could no longer perform the essential functions of his job.

Disability: Blindness

Accommodation Requested: Permanent assignment to switchboard and armory, reinstatement or transfer to another position at same rate of pay

Accommodation Required: No

Accommodation Adequate: N/A

Citation: *Miller v. Illinois Dep't of Corrections,* 107 F.3d 483, (7th Cir. 1997)

Statute: ADA

Explanation: After a car accident a **Corrections Officer** was rendered effectively blind. She asked to be reinstated after taking extensive medical leave but was not permitted to return. The court held that she could not perform the essential functions of her job, even though she could perform certain jobs within the officer rotation. She also indicated that she'd work another position in the prison, but wanted to maintain her higher officer salary. The court held that transferring her to a new position but paying her correction officer salary would have created a new position. The employer wasn't required to create a new position for the employee.

Disability: Colorblindness

Accommodation Requested: Position on police force

Accommodation Required: No

Accommodation Adequate: N/A

Citation: *Lekich v. Munic. Police Officers Educ. Training Cmsn*, 21 AD Cases (BNA) 1409 (E.D. Pa. 2009)

Statute: ADA; RA

Explanation: The Federal court dismissed an ADA suit brought by a **Police Applicant** who was rejected because of color vision impairment. The Court held that the applicant was not regarded as disabled and the lack of normal color vision is not a substantial limitation on the ability to see.

Disability: Inability to close right eyelid

Accommodation Requested: Use of a gas mask

Accommodation Required: Yes

Accommodation Adequate: Yes

Citation: *City of Cleveland v. Ohio Civil Rights Comm'n*, 98 Ohio App. 3d 243, 648 N.E.2d 516 (1994)

Statute: Ohio Civil Rights Commission § 4112-5-02(H)

Explanation: Court found that an employer's reliance on generalized medical standards to deny employment to a **Firefighter** with an eye condition was discriminatory without an individualized assessment. Though a condition preventing full closure of an eye is not debilitating, the employer's perception of it as such constituted discrimination under the Ohio Civil Rights Commission.

Disability: Loss of an eye

Accommodation Requested: Individual assessment of qualifying abilities of a firefighter position

Accommodation Required: Yes

Accommodation Adequate: Yes

Citation: *U.S. v. City of Pontiac*, (E.D. MI. 1994)

Statute: ADA

Explanation: A **Firefighter Applicant** with 14 years of experience, all necessary certifications, and excellent test scores was denied employment on the sole rationale that he did not meet a blanket requirement for certain vision conditions. The Court held that where a decision is made solely based on a broad standard of disabilities, it violates the ADA. Employers must engage in individual assessments if applicant s to determine whether or not they are qualified for the role.

Disability: Nyctalopia (Night-blindness)

Accommodation Requested: Modification of work schedule

Accommodation Required: Yes

Accommodation Adequate: Maybe

Citation: *Harrell v. Washington State*, 170 Wn.App. 386 (Wash. Ct. App 2012)

Statute: WLAD

Explanation: On-Call Counselor at McNeil Island Special Commitment Center who requested permanent day shifts to accommodate night blindness after being placed on swing shift schedule was not entitled to summary judgment in his favor where a jury could find that the State's offered reasonable accommodation was adequate. The CBA prevented the State from permanently modifying the work schedule of an on-call employee, and the Center offered the counselor the shifts he had requested whenever they arose.

Disability: Traumatic Mydriasis; Photophobia

Accommodation Requested: Excuse from overtime

Accommodation Required: No

Accommodation Adequate: N/A

Citation: *Watson v. Tex. Youth Comm'n*, 269 F. App'x 498 (5th Cir. 2008)

Statute: Rehabilitation Act

Explanation: A **Juvenile Corrections Officer**'s requests to be excused from overtime, due to his hyper-sensitivity to light, were not reasonable with respect to the duties of his job. The court found that corrections officers were expected to be available for longer shifts, and there was no way around it.

Disability: Vision Loss

Accommodation Requested: Driving exemption

Accommodation Required: Maybe

Accommodation Adequate: Maybe

Citation: *Rorrer v. City of Stow*, 29 AD Cases 447 (6th Cir. 2014)

Statute: ADA

Explanation: Vision-impaired city **Firefighter's** failure-to-accommodate claim could proceed to trial. Firefighter's request to be exempt from driving emergency vehicles might have been reasonable, the court found, given the evidence that such driving was a marginal rather than an essential job function. Also, the City failed to establish how such an exemption would necessarily impose an undue burden on the department.

Disability: Vision Loss: Substantial

Accommodation Requested: Reinstatement

Accommodation Required: No

Accommodation Adequate: N/A

Citation: *Miller v. Dept. of Corrections of State of Illinois*, 916 F.Supp. 863 (C.D.Ill.1996)

Statute: ADA

Explanation: Former city **Corrections Officer** brought ADA claims against the Department of Corrections after injuries sustained in a car accident caused her substantial loss of vision and her superiors gave her notice that she would not be allowed to return to duty. The court concluded that the officer must have had the ability to perform a wide range of tasks, most involving the supervision and surveillance of inmates, as an essential function of the correctional officer position, and because she cannot, she is not a qualified individual. Therefore, the ADA was not violated when the DOC terminated her employment.

Disability: Vision Loss: Stargardt's Disease (macular dystrophy)

Accommodation Requested: Device usage, relief from driving duties

Accommodation Required: Maybe **Accommodation Adequate:** Maybe

Citation: *Eldredge v. City of St. Paul*, 809 F. Supp. 2d 1011 (D. Minn. 2011) **Statute:** ADA

Explanation: Vision-impaired **Firefighter's** failure-to-accommodate claim could proceed to trial where the fire department had rejected his requests to be excused from driving department vehicles or to be allowed the use of a magnifying glass for necessary reading. The court noted that the City had not conducted a staffing assessment in order to determine whether the firefighter's requested driving exemption was unreasonable. It also explained that the City apparently misunderstood that he had only requested the use of a magnifying glass as an accommodation for reading fine print reading.

RESPIRATORY DISORDERS

Disability: Asthma

Accommodation Requested: Use of inhaler

Accommodation Required: Yes **Accommodation Adequate:** N/A

Citation: *Huber v. Howard County.*, 849 F. Supp. 407 (D. Md. 1994) **Statute:** ADA

Explanation: Discharged asthmatic probationary county **Firefighter's** case was dismissed because the court found that he did not show that the County's refusal to allow him to use his inhaler during endurance testing at firefighting academy was not job related or supported by legitimate safety concerns. Evidence indicated that the firefighter's brand of inhaler could not be used or stored near open flame and exposure to high temperatures could cause the device to burst. The court concluded that the County had reasonably determined that such device would be improper if used at the scene of a fire. In addition, the court ruled, the county was legitimately concerned with how inhaler could be used while the firefighter was wearing personal protective equipment, such as a helmet face guard, and gloves, as well as how long the inhaler would take to work.

Disability: Asthma

Accommodation Requested: Transfer to a smoke-free environment

Accommodation Required: Yes **Accommodation Adequate:** Yes

Citation: *Thorner-Green v. N.Y. City Dep't of Corr.*, 207 F. Supp. 2d 11 (E.D.N.Y. 2002) **Statute:** ADA

Explanation: A **Corrections Officer** with asthma requested several accommodations due to difficulty she was experiencing at work. The employer granted all three accommodation requests submitted by the employee, granting her two extended leaves and transferring her to a smoke-free section of the facility. The employee claimed that the location she was placed in was not truly smoke free, but she did not request any further transfers. The employer was not obligated to provide further transfers if they weren't requested.

Disability: Asthma

Accommodation Requested: Reassignment to a more ventilated work area

Accommodation Required: No

Accommodation Adequate: N/A

Citation: *Saunders v. Balt. Cty.*, 163 F. Supp. 2d 564 (D. Md. 2001)

Statute: ADA

Explanation: The court found that a **Corrections Officer** with asthma did not qualify as disable under the ADA because he failed to establish either that his asthma substantially limited his pursuit of a major life activity, or that his employer perceived his asthma to be a disability.

Disability: Asthma, Sarcoidosis

Accommodation Requested: Transfer to an available climate-controlled office

Accommodation Required: Yes

Accommodation Adequate: No

Citation: *Benaugh v. Ohio Civ. Rights Comm'n*, 278 F. App'x 501 (6th Cir. 2008)

Statute: Rehabilitation Act

Explanation: A **Senior Investigator for the Ohio Civil Rights Commission** was wrongfully denied proper accommodation for respiratory illness despite providing sufficient evidence that there was a causal relationship between her disability and the requested accommodation. Though the employer expressed initial willingness to accommodate, it was either unresponsive or dismissive when asked to elaborate or verify reasonable aspects of those offered accommodations

---

Disability: Chronic Obstructive Pulmonary Disease (COPD)

Accommodation Requested: Use of a self-contained breathing device, avoidance of smoke

Accommodation Required: No

Accommodation Adequate: N/A

Citation: 1995 EEOPUB LEXIS 2886

Statute: Rehabilitation Act

Explanation: A **Firefighter** forced to retire due to his COPD was deemed by the court to not be "disabled" under the Rehabilitation Act, not because COPD is not a debilitating condition, but because the nature of COPD immediately disqualifies a person from effectively operating as a firefighter. The condition directly impacts an individual's ability to perform all necessary functions of the job.

Disability: Severe allergy: cigarette smoke

Accommodation Requested: Designate police headquarter as non-smoking

Accommodation Required: Yes **Accommodation Adequate:** No

Citation: *Thursby v. City of Scranton*, 18 AD Cases 21 (M.D. Pa. 2006) **Statute:** ADA

Explanation: **Police Officer** with severe allergy to tobacco smoke and odors could proceed to trial with her failure-to-accommodate claim. Even though the City made non-smoking rooms available for her to use, there was evidence that she could not perform many of her job duties from the non-smoking rooms provided by the City. Additionally, although the City asked other officers "as a courtesy" to stop smoking when asked to do so by the officer with allergies, other officers continued to smoke despite her complaints. The court ruled that neither the collective-bargaining agreement with the police union nor its statutory duty to bargain prevented City from implementing a no-smoking policy that could have reasonably accommodated the officer.

Disability: Severe allergies

Accommodation Requested: Relocation to a different facility

Accommodation Required: Yes **Accommodation Adequate:** Maybe

Citation: *Matter of Cruz v. Shapiro*, 2016 NY Slip Op. 50363(U), 51 Misc. 3d 1203(A) (Sup. Ct.) **Statute:** ADA

Explanation: A **Probationary Corrections Officer** suffered from extreme allergic reactions likely caused by the facilities in which he worked, but which could not be verified. The allergies were deemed problematic enough to qualify as a disability, and relocation to another facility was considered reasonable accommodation (even where only 19% of alternate facilities were suitable).

Disability: Respiratory limitations resulting from lung cancer treatment

Accommodation Requested: Reinstatement, transfer some duties to other employees

Accommodation Required: No **Accommodation Adequate:** N/A

Citation: *Hummel v. County of* **Statute:** ADA

Saginaw, 40 Fed. Appx. 965 (6th Cir. 2002)

Explanation: Though a lung cancer survivor worked for nine months while she was being treated, after she completed treatment she was no longer qualified for her former position as a **Building Security Officer** through the Sheriff's Department. The employee had 25% of one of her lungs removed and she could no longer tolerate the same physical exertion that she could before surgery. The employee could not require the employer to transfer restraint and other responsibilities to other officers, as that was not a reasonable accommodation since restraint was an essential function of the position.

CIRCULATORY SYSTEM

Disability: Antiphospholipid Antibody Syndrome

Accommodation Requested: Minimizing stress (assignment to lower-stress dispatch desks, limit on consecutive days worked, avoidance of graveyard shifts)

Accommodation Required: Maybe

Accommodation Adequate: Yes

Citation: *Wilson v. Cty. of Orange*, 169 Cal. App. 4th 1185, 87 Cal. Rptr. 3d 439 (2009)

Statute: California Fair Employment and Housing Act (FEHA)

Explanation: A **Radio Dispatcher** received proper accommodation by assignment to alternative, lower stress desks and adjustments to her schedule despite some disagreement among supervisors as to the reasonableness of these modifications. Employer accommodated her disability in a timely and good-faith manner.

Disability: Blood clot (requiring anti-coagulants, physical altercation could cause employee to bleed out)

Accommodation Requested: Continue previous light duty

Accommodation Required: No

Accommodation Adequate: Yes

Citation: *Pickering v. City of Atlanta,* 75 F. Supp. 2d 1374 (N.D. Ga. 1999)

Statute: ADA

Explanation: A **Corrections Officer** at risk of bleeding out if she incurred a physical injury was placed on light duty for 2.5 years, effectively occupying a new position. It was not reasonable to require the employer to maintain the position created. She could not perform the essential functions of her job and was rightfully terminated.

Disability: Blood Thinning Condition

Accommodation Requested: Permanent assignment to control room

Accommodation Required: No

Accommodation Adequate: Yes

Citation: *Gasser v. Ramsey*, 11 AD Cases 280 (D.D.C. 2000)

Statute: ADA

Explanation: Former **Police Officer**, who was transferred to desk job allegedly because of his blood thinning condition, successfully showed that the transfer was due to his being "regarded as disabled" by his employer. The result of his transfer—ineligibility for overtime pay and lost promotional opportunity—was an adverse employment action in violation of the ADA.

Disability: Circulatory difficulty

Accommodation Requested: Permanent assignment to control room

Accommodation Required: No

Accommodation Adequate: Yes

Citation: *Hill v. Harper,* 6 F. Supp. 2d 540, (E.D. Va. 1998)

Statute: ADA

Explanation: A **Deputy Sheriff** could not rotate throughout all five of the mandatory positions in the jail due to a circulatory issue. When the ability to rotate throughout various posts at the jail is an essential job function, it is not reasonable to require the employer to permanently station the employee in one location as an accommodation, even when no other accommodations are available. This still holds true even if the employer permitted the employee to be permanently stationed there for three years prior.

Disability: Coronary Artery Disease

Accommodation Requested: Excused from emergency response

Accommodation Required: No

Accommodation Adequate: N/A

Citation: *Lusby v. Metropolitan Wash. Airports Auth.,* 1999 U.S. App. LEXIS 18428 (4th Cir. 1999)

Statute: ADA

Explanation: A **Firefighter/Assistant Fire Marshal** was diagnosed with coronary artery disease. He requested that he be excused from extreme exertion as an accommodation for his condition. The court held that emergency response is an essential function of the employee's job. Restructuring his responsibilities to excuse him from emergency response would eliminate an essential function of the employee's position. If he could not perform this essential function then he was not qualified for his job and the employer was justified in not providing that accommodation.

Disability: Heart condition

Accommodation Requested: Reinstatement

Accommodation Required: Yes **Accommodation Adequate:** No

Citation: *Hamlin v. Charter Twp. of Flint,* 165 F.3d 426 (6th Cir. 1999) **Statute:** ADA

Explanation: Because front-line firefighting is a non-essential function for the **Assistant Fire Chief** position, it was a reasonable accommodation to relieve the employee of that duty.

Disability: Heart problems (triple bypass surgery)

Accommodation Requested: Reinstatement of promotion to lieutenant

Accommodation Required: Yes **Accommodation Adequate:** N/A

Citation: *Kuntz v. City of New Have*n, CIVIL NO. N-90-480(JGM), 1993 U.S. Dist. LEXIS 20088 (D. Conn. Mar. 3, 1993) **Statute:** Rehabilitation Act

Explanation: A **Patrol Sergeant's** handicap was improperly taken into account in denying him a promotion to **Lieutenant**. The court found out that there were no new problematic responsibilities in the new position, and that it was potentially better suited to the employee than his current role considering the supervisory nature of Lieutenants.

Disability: Heart valve surgery; Increased risk of internal/external bleeding or hemorrhage

Accommodation Requested: Permanent reassignment to a noncontact position

Accommodation Required: Maybe **Accommodation Adequate:** N/A

Citation: *Evans v. Multnomah Cty. Sheriff's Office*, 184 Or. App. 733, 57 P.3d 211 (2002) **Statute:** ORS § 659A.112

Explanation: Oregon appellate court found that a **Corrections Officer's** request for reassignment to a position where he would not be exposed to potentially harmful contact with inmates was theoretically possible, and should be decided by a jury. Additionally, the essential duties of an employee should be considered with respect to a specific post, as opposed to a broader consideration of all the posts generally included in an employee's rotation.

Disability: Hypertension; Diabetes; Chronic Obstructive Pulmonary Disease

Accommodation Requested: Transfer, department vehicle, parking space

Accommodation Required: No **Accommodation Adequate:** Yes

Citation: *Raffaele v. City of New York*, 16 AD Cases 62 (E.D.N.Y. 2004) **Statute:** ADA

Explanation: The court concluded that the fire department did not fail to reasonably accommodate a former **Fire Prevention Inspector** when it denied his requests for: (1) transfer back to post that was close to home and his physician's office; (2) use of department vehicle; and (3) parking space at department headquarters. A doctor's letter accompanying his transfer request stated only that the employee had health conditions necessitating medical treatment and that transfer from his post made it more difficult to receive treatment, and the employer's alternative offered accommodation—use of employee's personal vehicle—was held to be sufficient.

Disability: Prinzmetal's Angina

Accommodation Requested: Light Duty Assignment

Accommodation Required: No **Accommodation Adequate:** N/A

Citation: *Shoemaker v. Pa. Human Relations Comm'n*, 160 Pa. Commw. 216, 634 A.2d 772 (1993) **Statute:** Pa. Stat. Ann. tit. 43, § 955(a)

Explanation: A 13-officer department was not required to accommodate a **Police Officer's** request for light-duty accommodation because it would require an undue burden of creating a new position.

Disability: Stroke: Multiple

Accommodation Requested: Assignment to light duty

Accommodation Required: Maybe **Accommodation Adequate:** Yes

Citation: *Swanson v. Village of Flossmoor*, 31 AD Cases 1560 (7th Cir. 2015) **Statute:** ADA

Explanation: A **Former Police Officer** did not have a valid claim under the ADA for failure to accommodate his limited physical abilities after he suffered two strokes. The officer was able to perform part-time work, and was not entitled to his preferred reasonable accommodation of light duty. His employer had reasonably accommodated him by permitting him to remain on its health plan and work a part-time schedule.

ENDOCRINE

Disability: Diabetes

Accommodation Requested: Transfer to new station

Accommodation Required: Maybe **Accommodation Adequate:** Maybe

Citation: *Gilday v. Mecosta County*, 7 AD Cases 348 (6th Cir. 1997) **Statute:** ADA

Explanation: Discharged diabetic **EMT's** evidence creates factual question supporting his ADA claims that his diabetes constitutes a disability and that his employer should have granted his request for the reasonable accommodation of transferring him to a less chaotic station, which would have allowed to maintain the regimen that controls his diabetes. The court held it possible, to be determined by a jury, that he was a qualified person with a disability.

Disability: Diabetes

Accommodation Requested: Modification of work schedule

Accommodation Required: Maybe **Accommodation Adequate:** Maybe

Citation: *Lee v. District of Columbia*, 920 F. Supp. 2d 127 (D.D.C. 2013) **Statute:** ADA

Explanation: Diabetic city **Corrections Officer** may proceed with ADA failure-to-accommodate claim after he was fired for sleeping at work. He fell asleep 90 minutes after he was denied regular lunch break. The court cited the evidence that he was substantially limited in his ability to stay alert when he missed meals and that he frequently requested meal breaks because of his diabetes and its impact on his alertness. The court rejected the City's argument that the officer had to formally request accommodation or comply with fixed procedures to provide notice of his need for an accommodation in advance of his citation for the rule violation.

Disability: Diabetes

Accommodation Requested: To carry medicine and medical equipment on self during training; placement of proper medical disposal bins on the premises

Accommodation Required: Yes **Accommodation Adequate:** Yes

Citation: *Barry v. Nebraska*, 2016 U.S. Dist. 78566 (D. Neb. Jun 16, 2016) **Statute:** ADA

Explanation: Diabetic **Corrections Trainee** was wrongfully denied her right to carry her diabetes medicine and equipment during training. Department of Corrections was required to keep a designated and medically-cleared disposal bin for the medical refuse of the trainee.

Disability: Diabetes

Accommodation Requested: Altered shifts

Accommodation Required: Maybe **Accommodation Adequate:** No

Citation: *Szarawara v. County of Montgomery,* 2013 U.S. Dist. LEXIS 90386, (E.D. Pa. 2013) **Statute:** ADA

Explanation: A **Dispatcher** was experiencing health problems from diabetes, which were exacerbated by his work schedule. He requested and suggested a number of accommodations in order to sleep better and only work days as his physician suggested, but the employer refused because a better sleep schedule would help anyone, not just the plaintiff. "The Court cannot say that Defendant was relieved of its obligations under the ADA because Plaintiff's doctor suggested alternatives to Plaintiff's requested accommodation that would also mitigate the effects of his medical conditions." Furthermore, just because a particular accommodation would also benefit a non-disabled person does not mean that the accommodation is not related to the employee's disability.

Disability: Diabetes

Accommodation Requested: Re-hire as permit clerk

Accommodation Required: Yes **Accommodation Adequate:** Yes

Citation: *Castellani v. Bucks County Municipality,* 351 Fed. Appx. 774 (3d Cir. 2009) **Statute:** ADA

Explanation: After a **Dispatcher** failed to return from medical leave, the county terminated her. She requested an accommodation after her termination. However, she had no evidence that there were any open positions at her time of termination and she conceded that she could not return to her dispatcher position.

Disability: Diabetes

Accommodation Requested: Opportunity to eat food and regulate glucose levels, reinstatement into training

Accommodation Required: Maybe **Accommodation Adequate:** Maybe

Citation: *United States v. Miss. Dep't of Pub. Safety*, 309 F. Supp. 2d 837 (S.D. Miss. 2004) **Statute:** ADA

Explanation: Court found that Highway **Safety Patrol Cadet's** diabetes qualified as a disability under the ADA because of its effect on the "major life activity" of eating, and held that requests for additional food in order to regulate blood sugar levels constituted requests for reasonable accommodation. Additionally, court found that reinstatement might be reasonable accommodation because a jury could find that the employee's outburst to an officer—the reason for his expulsion—was a direct result of his unaccommodated diabetes.

Disability: Diabetes

Accommodation Requested: Retesting

Accommodation Required: Yes

Accommodation Adequate: Yes

Citation: *Gonzales v. City of New Braunfels*, 176 F.3d 834 (5th Cir. 1999)

Statute: ADA

Explanation: A **Police Officer** discharged after failing firearms and driving requalification tests claimed he was entitled to a retest or transfer to a job as an evidence technician. The court found these requested accommodations would not have been a reasonable: 1) driving is an essential function of police officer position, and a driver with insulin-dependent diabetes poses a direct threat to health and safety of others as matter of law; 2) an evidence technician must be commissioned officer, and in order to be a commissioned officer one must be both firearms and driving certified.

Disability: Diabetes

Accommodation Requested: A "second chance"

Accommodation Required: Yes

Accommodation Adequate: Yes

Citation: *Siefken v. Village of Arlington Heights,* 65 F.3d 664 (7th Cir. 1995)

Statute: ADA

Explanation: A **Police Officer** had a diabetic reaction, causing him to become disoriented, lose his memory, and speed recklessly around in his patrol car. The court determined that the department had already accommodated the officer by permitting him to monitor and control his diabetes. The court upheld his termination, despite the officer's request for another chance, as he failed to monitor his condition.

Disability: Diabetes

Accommodation Requested: Ability to enter police force

Accommodation Required: Yes

Accommodation Adequate: No

Citation: *Bombrys v. City of Toledo,* 849 F. Supp. 1210 (N.D. Ohio 1993) **Statute:** ADA

Explanation: Permitting diabetics to enter the police force and take a few minutes a day to test their blood sugar levels is reasonable. The police force did not prohibit other **Police Officers** with potentially dangerous conditions, such as epilepsy, form entering the force. Officers who acquired diabetes while on the force were not required to quit. Allowing an officer to carry testing materials, medicine, and extra food did not disrupt the law enforcement activities of the officers. The court therefore held that there could be no blanket exclusion of diabetics from entering the department.

Disability: Diabetes

Accommodation Requested: Ability to become FBI agent

Accommodation Required: No **Accommodation Adequate:** N/A

Citation: *Raspa v. Office of Sheriff of Cty. of Gloucester*, 191 N.J. 323, 924 A.2d 435 (2007) **Statute:** Rehabilitation Act

Explanation: The FBI is not required to create permanent light-duty positions for diabetic **FBI Agents**. There is a risk that a diabetic could experience an unexpected hypoglycemic attack, putting themselves and others at risk. It is too dangerous to keep them in the field, but there are no permanent light-duty positions so it is permissible to exclude diabetics from the FBI.

Disability: Diabetes; High blood pressure; High cholesterol; Coronary Artery Disease

Accommodation Requested: Reinstatement to full duty

Accommodation Required: No **Accommodation Adequate:** N/A

Citation: *Lui v. City & County of San Francisco*, 211 Cal. App. 4th 962 (2012) **Statute:** ADA

Explanation: After a **Police Officer** suffered a major heart attack, he retired after being told that there were no administrative positions available that did not require strenuous physical duties. The officer subsequently sued the City, claiming disability discrimination and failure to reasonably accommodate his condition. This court held that such strenuous physical activities were "essential job functions," even in administrative positions. The City needed to be able to deploy administrative officers in the field when emergencies occur. Both the discrimination and failure to accommodate claims were rejected.

Disability: Diabetes; Kidney disease

Accommodation Requested: Transfer to a position with equal pay to what the employee was making in her current position

Accommodation Required: Yes

Accommodation Adequate: Yes

Citation: *Fry v. Sheahan,* 2009 U.S. Dist. LEXIS 70630 (N.D. Ill. 2009)

Statute: ADA

Explanation: The **Jail Administrative Assistant** couldn't perform the essential functions of her job and was limited in her ability to stand for extended periods of time. The employee was offered a position that was lower than hers and would pay her $7,000 less a year. She initially turned the position down but this was an adequate accommodation. Furthermore, the employer wasn't required to continually give the responsibilities she couldn't do to other employees.

Disability: Diabetes; Angina Pectoris: Severe

Accommodation Requested: Reinstatement as a police officer

Accommodation Required: No

Accommodation Adequate: Yes

Citation: *Muhammad v. New Orleans Police Dep't,* 791 So. 2d 788, 2001 La. App. LEXIS 1792, 2000-1034 (La. Ct. App. 2001)

Statute: ADA

Explanation: The employee was completely unable to function as a **Police Officer** and the department began termination proceedings. At the same time the department attempted to find the employee work in another position with the city. He was offered the position of truck driver but due to his medication he could not accept the position. They terminated him and the court upheld his termination, determining that the city had made a reasonable effort to accommodate the employee.

Disability: Obesity, heart problems

Accommodation Requested: Limited assignment to "light duty" positions

Accommodation Required: No

Accommodation Adequate: Yes

Citation: *McDonald v. Department of Corrections,* 880 F. Supp. 1416 (D. Kan. 1995)

Statute: ADA

Explanation: An overweight **Corrections Officer** suffered from heart problems. His doctor was not sure when his condition would improve. The court held that the employer was not required to limit him to light duty positions such as watchtower and clothing issue. The defendant made and adequate showing that such an accommodation would be an undue hardship and the employee failed to provide any evidence that the accommodation problem could present an issue of fact.

Disability: Obesity: Morbid

Accommodation Requested: Hire applicant

Accommodation Required: Maybe **Accommodation Adequate:** N/A

Citation: *Cook v. State of RI*, 783 F.Supp. 1569, (D.R.I. 1992) **Statute:** Rehab Act

Explanation: An overweight former **Institutional Attendant** applying for a similar position at the Rhode Island Department of Mental Health, Retardation and Hospitals filed suit against MHRH for refusing to hire her after its examining physician refused to approve her application when she failed to lose the weight. The court held that, rather than providing an accommodation, MHRH required Cook to reduce or eliminate her alleged handicap in order to be hired. Therefore, the court denied MHRH's motion to dismiss, determining that the applicant was entitled to relief under the Federal Rehab. Act as a "handicapped individual."

Disability: Obesity; Hypertension

Accommodation Requested: Steady day shift, swapping shifts

Accommodation Required: Maybe **Accommodation Adequate:** N/A

Citation: *Honey v. County of Rockland,* 200 F. Supp. 2d 311 (S.D.N.Y. 2002) **Statute:** ADA

Explanation: After her doctor determined that her frequently rotating shift aggravated her health problems, a **Dispatcher** requested accommodation. She was accommodated for a while, but after bringing suit her accommodations were removed. The court permitted the question of failure to accommodate to continue to trial.

Disability: Grave's Disease (hyperactive thyroid)

Accommodation Requested: No contact with inmates, permanent light-duty assignment

Accommodation Required: No **Accommodation Adequate:** N/A

Citation: *Raspa v. Office of Sheriff of Cty. of Gloucester*, 191 N.J. 323, 924 A.2d 435 (2007) **Statute:** New Jersey Law Against Discrimination

Explanation: It was unreasonable for a **Correctional Officer** to never have contact with inmates. Temporary suspensions of the duty are reasonable, but removing the responsibility entirely does not comport with the nature of a corrections officer.

NEUROLOGICAL DISORDERS

Disability: Brain injury leading to mental, emotional, and physical difficulties

Accommodation Requested: Promotion

Accommodation Required: Yes

Accommodation Adequate: Yes

Citation: *Land v. Washington County*, 243 F.3d 1093 (8th Cir. 2001)

Statute: ADA

Explanation: A **Corrections Officer** twice requested and received accommodations, but was passed over multiple times for promotions. The officer believed that he did not get the promotions because he was not adequately accommodated. The court found that, because the employer had accommodated the requests that had been made, they had made reasonable accommodations for the employee and he simply was no longer qualified.

Disability: Dyslexia

Accommodation Requested: Excuse form portions of Correctional Officer certification training

Accommodation Required: No

Accommodation Adequate: N/A

Citation: *Burke v. Virginia*, 938 F. Supp. 320 (E.D. Va. 1996)

Statute: ADA

Explanation: Employee hired as a **Correctional Officer** and sent to training to be certified was declined certification after repeatedly failing portions of the training, which he later attributed to his dyslexia. Court held that employer offered numerous reasonable accommodations—similarly paying positions that did not require certification—and rightfully considered the officer's disability a hindrance to his ability to perform the essential functions of the job.

Disability: Dyslexia

Accommodation Requested: Prove "reader" to help him during entrance exam

Accommodation Required: No

Accommodation Adequate: N/A

Citation: *Bageris v. Brandon Twp.*, 264 Mich. App. 156 (Mich. Ct. App. 2004)

Statute: Michigan's Persons With Disabilities Civil Rights Act

Explanation: A **Part-Time Firefighter** was required to take a written test as part of his application to become a full-time firefighter. He asked to have a reader due to difficulties with test-taking. He was not provided with a reader. The court held that simply stating that he had difficulty with tests was not adequate notice by the firefighter to the employer of his disability.

Disability: Dyslexia: Inability to read at 12th-grade level

Accommodation Requested: Permit materials to be read to employee by family and colleagues, eliminate housewatch duty

Accommodation Required: No

Accommodation Adequate: N/A

Citation: *DiPompo v. W. Point Military Acad.*, 770 F. Supp. 887 (S.D.N.Y. 1991)

Statute: Rehabilitation Act

Explanation: A **Structural Firefighter** unable to meet the minimum reading requirements of West Point firefighters was denied accommodation by the court because the measures necessary to accommodate his disability were unreasonably burdensome.

Disability: Multiple Sclerosis

Accommodation Requested: Reassignment to avoid tasks requiring controlled balance: climbing ladders and driving emergency vehicles.

Accommodation Required: Yes

Accommodation Adequate: Yes

Citation: *Davis v. City of Grapevine*, 188 S.W.3d 748 (Tex. App. 2006)

Statute: Texas Commission on Human Rights Act, Tex. Lab. Cod Ann. § 21.00-.556 (1996)

Explanation: Court held that a **Former Firefighter** with MS was "disabled" under the meaning of the statute—he struggled to perform acts requiring heightened physical control, such as climbing and running—and that the city's "consideration" of him for a suitable vacant position (a letter of recommendation) did not rise to the level of "reassignment" to a vacant position (an active effort on the part of the employer to secure employment) as required by the Tenth Circuit.

Disability: Multiple Sclerosis

Accommodation Requested: Job restructuring

Accommodation Required: Maybe

Accommodation Adequate: Maybe

Citation: *Miller v. Benton County*, 27 AD Cases 1413 (D. Minn. 2013)

Statute: ADA

Explanation: Former county **Jail Sergeant's** failure-to-accommodate claim could proceed to trial. The sergeant had Multiple Sclerosis and was provided an informal accommodation of control center assignment without inmate contact during MS exacerbations. Eventually, the informal accommodation was discontinued, at which point the sergeant began having attendance problems. The court concluded that such attendance problems alone were not sufficient evidence that she was not entitled to a reasonable accommodation.

Disability: Multiple Sclerosis

Accommodation Requested: Overtime scheduling

Accommodation Required: Yes

Accommodation Adequate: Yes

Citation: *Cormier v. City of Meriden*, 420 F. Supp. 2d 11 (D. Conn. 2006)

Statute: ADA

Explanation: City **Public Safety Dispatcher** with Multiple Sclerosis was medically restricted to work no more than 12 consecutive hours, but could not proceed with her ADA failure-to-accommodate claim. Court found that the City's proposed accommodation—allowing the dispatcher to accept any four-hour overtime shifts and any eight-hour overtime shift on days that she was not scheduled to work—did not pose a risk of violating her 12-hour work restriction and was thus reasonable.

Disability: Multiple Sclerosis

Accommodation Requested: Transfer to another position

Accommodation Required: Maybe

Accommodation Adequate: Yes

Citation: *Doner v. City of Rockford,* 77 Fed. Appx. 898 (7th Cir. 2003)

Statute: ADA; Rehabilitation Act

Explanation: Multiple Sclerosis rendered a **Police Officer** incapable of apprehending suspects. After learning that the officer would never be able to walk again, the Deputy Chief terminated him. The court determined that, because he could not apprehend suspects, the officer was incapable of performing an essential function of the job. The officer also failed to point out any specific vacant position he could have been moved to.

Disability: Multiple Sclerosis

Accommodation Requested: Job restructuring, assignment to a vacant position

Accommodation Required: No

Accommodation Adequate: N/A

Citation: *Frazier v. Simmons,* 254 F.3d 1247 (10th Cir. 2001)

Statute: ADA

Explanation: Due to MS, a **Corrections Investigator** had lost 50% of his vision, had balance problems, and lost strength in his hands. This kept him from being able to restrain prisoners and safely handle a firearm. He sought to have some of the essential functions of his job transferred to others or to be transferred to vacant positions that he was not qualified for. He was terminated. The court held that the employer had acted reasonably, as they were not required to shift essential functions of the job or transfer him to a position that was not qualified and would essentially be a promotion.

Disability: Multiple Sclerosis

Accommodation Requested: Light duty

Accommodation Required: Yes

Accommodation Adequate: Yes

Citation: *Maynard v. Nygren,* 2000 U.S. Dist. LEXIS 9208 (N.D. Ill. 2000)

Statute: ADA

Explanation: A **Corrections Officer** with MS requested light duty in order to continue working despite his condition The employer refused, as no light duty assignments existed. An employer does not have to provide an accommodation in the form of a light duty assignment if no light duty assignments are available.

Disability: Multiple Sclerosis

Accommodation Requested: Transfer to civilian position

Accommodation Required: Yes

Accommodation Adequate: Yes

Citation: *Barzellone v. City of Tulsa,* 2000 U.S. App. LEXIS 5987 (10th Cir. 2000)

Statute: ADA

Explanation: After being convicted for a number of charges, including reckless driving and violating a protection order, a **Police Officer** was terminated. She stated that her actions had stemmed from her impairments and provided a doctor's note on the matter. She claimed she had not been accommodated, but the court noted that the city had offered her positions that she turned down and the officer had failed to contribute to the interactive process of determining an accommodation, relieving the city of liability.

Disability: Epilepsy

Accommodation Requested: Transfer to new, currently-occupied, role

Accommodation Required: Maybe

Accommodation Adequate: N/A

Citation: *Scheer v. City of Cedar Rapids*, 956 F. Supp. 1496 (N.D. Iowa 1997)

Statute: ADA

Explanation: An **Airport Safety Officer** recovering from an epilepsy diagnoses—proceeding through required waiting periods before being allowed to drive and engage in other activities—requested a changing list of accommodations, before asking for a new shift of his current job. The court held that, because there was no opening available for that shift, the employer was not required to transfer the employee.

Disability: Epilepsy

Accommodation Requested: Non-rotating shift

Accommodation Required: Yes **Accommodation Adequate:** N/A

Citation: *Dicksey v. New Hanover County Sheriff's Dep't*, 522 F. Supp. 2d 742 (E.D.N.C. 2007) **Statute:** ADA

Explanation: Epileptic former **Deputy Sheriff** could not proceed with his failure-to-accommodate claim because he was not a "qualified individual" under the ADA. Although he argued that he would be qualified for a front desk position if the county provided his requested accommodation for a non-rotating day shift assignment, he was unable to meet state standards requiring that he be seizure-free and was therefore unable to perform essential job functions requiring uninterrupted vigilance. Additionally, assigning him to permanent day shift, the court ruled, would unduly burden staff required to work his night shifts. Finally, he could not show that he would be seizure-free even if he were accommodated.

Disability: Epilepsy

Accommodation Requested: Transfer to a nonhazardous position

Accommodation Required: Yes **Accommodation Adequate:** Yes

Citation: *Salmon Pineiro v. Lehman*, 653 F. Supp. 483 (D.P.R. 1987) **Statute:** Rehabilitation Act

Explanation: Epileptic **Criminal Investigator** for the Naval Investigative Services suffered seizures that were considered a significant risk within his role. He was offered an alternative position as accommodation for his disability but declined to job. Employer's ensuing termination was therefore appropriate.

Disability: Epilepsy, frequent nausea

Accommodation Requested: Duty limited to specific positions

Accommodation Required: Maybe **Accommodation Adequate:** N/A

Citation: *Vazquez v. Bedsole,* 888 F. **Statute:** ADA

Supp. 727 (E.D.N.C. 1995)

Explanation: After sustaining an injury that led to permanent problems and a number of surgeries, the plaintiff was demoted from **Deputy Sheriff**. The sheriff believed that the employee could no longer perform her duties. Plaintiff identified a number of positions she could hold despite her injury, and the court held that she could proceed with her claim.

Disability: Seizures

Accommodation Requested: Limited duty for five year wait period required after seizures

Accommodation Required: No

Accommodation Adequate: N/A

Citation: *Coleman v. Pa. State Police,* 2014 U.S. App. LEXIS 5237 (3d Cir. 2014)

Statute: ADA; Rehabilitation Act

Explanation: The court determined that a **Trooper Cadet** could not demand five years of limited duty when, pursuant to a department policy, he was required to wait five years after experiencing seizures to return to full duty. The court ultimately held that the fact that he was subject to the wait period and had not completed his training rendered him unqualified for the position of officer and therefore not protected by state statute.

Disability: Post-concussive Syndrome; Seizure Disorder; Post-traumatic Epilepsy

Accommodation Requested: Promotion

Accommodation Required: Yes

Accommodation Adequate: N/A

Citation: *Morris v. City of New York,* 153 F. Supp. 2d 494 (S.D.N.Y. 2002)

Statute: ADA

Explanation: After **Police Officer** was denied a promotion to sergeant, the officer brought an ADA claim against the City, alleging that he was denied a promotion as a result of his record of disability in violation of the ADA and the NYSHRL. The Court held that given the City's overt references to the officer's sick record, and evidence of the City's knowledge that the officer's sick days were closely related to his disability, a jury might reasonably infer that the City's decision not to promote the officer was motivated, at least in part, by discrimination on the basis of a record of disability.

Disability: Polyneuropathy

Accommodation Requested: Assignment to court room duty

Accommodation Required: Maybe

Accommodation Adequate: Yes

Citation: *Shannon v. Cook County Sheriff's Merit Bd.,* 1998 U.S. Dist. LEXIS 4859 (N.D. Ill. 1998)

Statute: ADA

Explanation: A **Deputy Sheriff** required sedentary work as accommodation—a desk job recording information in a notebook—, but requested alternative accommodation in a less-sedentary role— assignment to a court room as a Deputy Sheriff. The ADA does not require Plaintiff's employer to grant Plaintiff's request for a particular job. Defendants need only reasonably accommodate her requirement for a sedentary job.

MENTAL OR PSYCHOLOGICAL DISORDERS

Disability: Anxiety

Accommodation Requested: N/A

Accommodation Required: Maybe

Accommodation Adequate: N/A

Citation: *Lane v. Clark County*, 2015 AD Cases 183841 (9th Cir. 2015)

Statute: ADA

Explanation: A **Juvenile Detention Center Cook** did not have a valid claim under the ADA that his employer had failed to accommodate his anxiety. The cook's anxiety prevented him from performing the essential functions of his job with or without reasonable accommodation, and he did not engage in the interactive process or offer potential reasonable accommodations.

Disability: Anxiety; Stress

Accommodation Requested: Indefinite leave

Accommodation Required: No

Accommodation Adequate: Yes

Citation: *Hopkins v. City of Bothell,* 2003 Wash. App. LEXIS 1151 (Wash. Ct. App. 2003)

Statute: ADA

Explanation: A **Police Officer** with severe anxiety and stress took leave. He continued to be completely unable to work, and was told to either retire or he would be terminated. The officer could not provide an expected return date. Even though the employee had unused medical leave remaining when he was asked to retire, the employer did not have to let him use the entirely of his leave. His doctor indicated that it was unclear when he would be well enough to return, and the department was not required to grant him indefinite leave.

Disability: Anxiety; Depression

Accommodation Requested: Reassignment

Accommodation Required: No

Accommodation Adequate: N/A

Citation: *Hill v. Walker*, 737 F. 3d 1209 (8th Cir. 2013)

Statute: ADA; FMLA; FLSA

Explanation: Suffering from depression and anxiety from her job, an Arkansas **State Agency Employee** was terminated because of her absence during a stressful case. While she suffers a recognized disability, the court held that, "because the service worker could not perform the essential functions of her position, she failed to create a genuine issue for trial on a claim of discrimination under the ADA." Thus, the court dismissed the claim.

Disability: Anxiety; Depression

Accommodation Requested: Excuse from mandatory overtime

Accommodation Required: Maybe

Accommodation Adequate: N/A

Citation: *Reeder v. Cty. of Wayne*, 2016 U.S. Dist. LEXIS 46243 (E.D. Mich. Apr. 6, 2016)

Statute: ADA

Explanation: A **Police Officer** suffering from depression and anxiety—causing a lack of appetite, restless nights, and an inability to work more than eight hours a day—was considered substantially limited enough to qualify as disabled under the ADA. Though an inability to work overtime is not a disability, an inability to sleep or eat is.

Disability: Anxiety; Depression; Insomnia

Accommodation Requested: Reduction of shift length to 8 hours

Accommodation Required: Maybe

Accommodation Adequate: N/A

Citation: *Williams v. Ala. Dep't of Corr.,* 29 AD Cases 1280 (N.D. Ala. 2014)

Statute: ADA

Explanation: A **Correctional Officer** had repeated issues with calling in due to medication he was taking for his problems. He requested his shifts be shortened to accommodate him, but the prison refused. The court permitted the accommodation question to move forward to trial.

Disability: Attention Deficit Hyperactivity Disorder (ADHD)

Accommodation Requested: Return to active duty

Accommodation Required: Maybe **Accommodation Adequate:** Maybe

Citation: *Weaving v. City of Hillsboro*, 26 AD Cases 229 (D. Or. 2012) **Statute:** ADA

Explanation: Hillsboro Oregon **Police Sergeant** with attention deficit hyperactivity disorder was not entitled to summary judgment in his favor on his failure-to-accommodate claim, nor was the City on its asserted defenses to his suit. The City argued that his request for return to active duty was not reasonable and may have posed an undue hardship, citing his alleged misconduct when interacting with his subordinates, "described by numerous individuals … as tyrannical, unapproachable, non-communicative, belittling and demeaning, threatening/intimidating, arrogant and vindictive" which had resulted in harassment complaints.

Disability: Attention Deficit Hyperactivity Disorder (ADHD)

Accommodation Requested: Adjustments to promotions test: time, structure, etc.

Accommodation Required: No **Accommodation Adequate:** N/A

Citation: *Knapp v. City of Columbus*, 192 F. App'x 323 (6th Cir. 2006) **Statute:** ADA, Rehabilitation Act, Ohio handicap discrimination law

Explanation: Plaintiff **Firefighters** failed to show that ADHD was a "Disability" under the ADA, due to the effectiveness of their medication (Ritalin) in treating and minimalizing the impact the disorder had on their daily lives.

Disability: Bipolar Disorder

Accommodation Requested: Reinstatement conditioned on medication monitoring

Accommodation Required: No **Accommodation Adequate:** N/A

Citation: *Hogarth v. Thornburgh,* 833 F. Supp. 1077 (S.D.N.Y. 1993) **Statute:** Rehabilitation Act

Explanation: The FBI did not have to re-hire a former **FBI Clerk** who had psychotic episodes due to his bipolar disorder. He had suffered recurring delusions and had at times lost touch with reality. Given the sensitive nature of the information he would be dealing with as a communications operator the FBI was not obligated to give him his job back, and was not obligated to monitor his medication consumption to ensure he was complying with his treatment

---

Disability: Bipolar Disorder, Obsessive Compulsive Disorder

Accommodation Requested: Transfer to a different department, removal of a past corrective action for his record

Accommodation Required: No

Accommodation Adequate: N/A

Citation: *Scherer v. GE Capital Corp.*, 59 F. Supp. 2d 1132 (D. Kan. 1999)

Statute: ADA

Explanation: A **Fraud Investigator** failed to show how his disability substantially limited a major life activity—it was effectively controlled through medication—as required for coverage under the ADA, and thus was not entitled to reasonable accommodation by his employer.

Disability: Claustrophobia

Accommodation Requested: Reassignment

Accommodation Required: Yes

Accommodation Adequate: No

Citation: *Hall v. Claussen,* 6 Fed. Appx. 655, (10th Cir. 2001)

Statute: ADA

Explanation: While an employer is not required to promote an employee in order to accommodate them, they must look for positions that would constitute a lateral transfer and determine that none are available before offering a position that would constitute a demotion. Furthermore, even though the court did not ultimately determine that the employee's claustrophobia was a disability, the fact that the employer tried to reassign a **Deputy Sheriff** to a position that triggered problems with that fear could be evaluated in determining whether or not the accommodation was reasonable.

Disability: Depression

Accommodation Requested: N/A

Accommodation Required: No

Accommodation Adequate: N/A

Citation: *Ballinger v. City of Fort Wayne*, 2015 AD Cases 190988 (N.D. Ind. 2015)

Statute: ADA

Explanation: After **Police Officer** disclosed his depression, the officer was placement on light duty pending mental health fitness-for-duty evaluation. The record indicated that the officer was engaged in a pattern of unusual behavior over an extended period of time. The Court held that his retaliation claim fails because he did not show a causal connection between his attorney's letter and the alleged "retaliatory treatment."

Disability: Depression; perceived mental impairment/fear of fire

Accommodation Requested: Reinstatement to fire suppression unit

Accommodation Required: No **Accommodation Adequate:** N/A

Citation: *City of Houston v. Proler,* 29 AD Cases 1721 (Tex. 2014) **Statute:** ADA

Explanation: The court held that the fire department was not required to provide a **Firefighter** with any accommodations, as his disqualification from one job was insufficient to constitute the impairment of a major life activity and he was therefore not disabled.

Disability: Depression; Hypertension

Accommodation Requested: Formal notice of why he received his requested shifts

Accommodation Required: No **Accommodation Adequate:** Yes

Citation: *Krocka v. Bransfield,* 969 F. Supp. 1073 (N.D. Ill. 1997) **Statute:** ADA

Explanation: A **Police Officer** received the shifts he requested as an accommodation. The employer was not required to provide him with formal notice of the accommodation or why he had been receiving the shifts he wanted. The fact that he got the accommodation was enough and he was not entitled to "official" notification.

Disability: Depression

Accommodation Requested: Reinstatement as a police officer

Accommodation Required: Yes **Accommodation Adequate:** No

Citation: *Department of Pub. Safety & Corrections, Office of State Police v. Mensman,* 671 So.2d 319 (La. Ct. App. 1996) **Statute:** Appeal of State Police Commission decision

Explanation: A **Police Officer** repeatedly took unreported, unauthorized breaks and would fail to report for duty. His superiors would not accommodate his attempts to engage in therapy and they attempted to fire him. The court upheld the Commission's decision to reduce his termination to a suspension.

Disability: Depression

Accommodation Requested: Reassignment

Accommodation Required: No **Accommodation Adequate:** N/A

Citation: *Bohannon v. Dept. of Homeland Security*, 99 M.S.P.R. 307 (2005)

Statute: ADA

Explanation: MSPB affirms an arbitrator's holding that a **Security Employee**, who was terminated for poor performance, was not "disabled" and entitled to an accommodation. Moreover, an employee must first show that a reasonable accommodation is possible and a causal connection between his disability and the charged misconduct.

Disability: Depression

Accommodation Requested: Reinstatement, light duty

Accommodation Required: No

Accommodation Adequate: N/A

Citation: *Md. Comm'n on Human Rels. v. Mayor & Balt.,* 86 Md. App. 167 (Md. Ct. Spec. App. 1991)

Statute: Rehabilitation Act

Explanation: A **Police Officer** expressed suicidal ideas to another officer while off duty. She was put on leave, evaluated by doctors, and deemed not fit to be an officer. One officer suggested she be placed on the phones, but the court held that such an accommodation would be so drastic as to fundamentally alter the employee's essential duties, which they were not required to do.

Disability: Depression

Accommodation Requested: Reassignment

Accommodation Required: Maybe

Accommodation Adequate: N/A

Citation: *Stevens v. Ill. Dep't of Corr.*, 32 AD Cases 579 (C.D. Ill. 2015)

Statute: ADA

Explanation: An Illinois **State Correctional Officer** may proceed with ADA discrimination and retaliation claims based on his discharge and delayed reinstatement after he was hospitalized for depression and requested accommodation. Employer could have waived state bans on firearm ownership by those hospitalized for mental illness.

Disability: Depression; Mixed Personality Disorder

Accommodation Requested: Reassignment

Accommodation Required: No

Accommodation Adequate: N/A

Citation: *Lang v. City of Maplewood,* 574 N.W.2d 451 (Minn. Ct. App. 1998)

Statute: Minnesota Human Rights Act (MHRA)

Explanation: After he was diagnosed with a mental disorder and brain malformation (which was treated but did not fully remedy his problems), a **Police Officer** was terminated. Doctors stated that he was permanently incapable of functioning as an officer. He applied for and received benefits, but challenged his termination on the grounds that he should have been given another position. The court held, "No reasonable accommodation would have permitted Lang to perform his job as a police officer. The City is not required under MHRA to provide alternative employment for Lang."

Disability: Depression; Anxiety

Accommodation Requested: Additional training, counseling

Accommodation Required: Yes **Accommodation Adequate:** Yes

Citation: *Lucke v. Multnomah County*, 21 AD Cases 538 (D. Or. 2008) **Statute:** ADA

Explanation: The court found that Multnomah County had reasonably accommodated a former county sheriff's **Corrections Deputy** with depression and anxiety. Within one day of learning of her impairments, the county contacted the deputy regarding her need for accommodation, she received her requested accommodations of additional training, and she was offered counseling.

Disability: Depression

Accommodation Requested: Leave of absence, job transfer

Accommodation Required: Yes **Accommodation Adequate:** Maybe

Citation: *Williams v. Philadelphia Housing Auth. Police Dept.*, 380 F.3d 751 (3d Cir. 2004) **Statute:** ADA

Explanation: A housing authority may have failed to reasonably accommodate a former **Police Officer** who was restricted from carrying a firearm because of his depression. The court denied the employer's motion for dismissal, finding that a jury might appropriately conclude that the housing authority's failure to transfer him to a job in radio or the training unit was a failure to reasonably accommodate.

Disability: Depression

Accommodation Requested: Modification of work schedule

Accommodation Required: Yes **Accommodation Adequate:** N/A

Citation: *Brown v. City of Tucson*, 336 F.3d 1181 (9th Cir. 2003) **Statute:** ADA

Explanation: Former **Police Detective** instructed by supervisor to discontinue prescribed medications had a valid claim for an actionable threat qualifying as "interference" under ADA. The detective had been excused from nighttime call-out duty as an accommodation for her depression. But her supervisor later demanded that she stop taking her medications and instead perform nighttime call-out duty *or* face demotion or forced retirement. The Ninth Circuit ruled that ordering an employee to choose between foregoing previously granted accommodation or face adverse employment consequences cannot be interpreted as a reasonable effort to determine an appropriate accommodation.

Disability: Depression; perceived mental impairment at base of cranium

Accommodation Requested: Reinstatement to fire suppression unit

Accommodation Required: No

Accommodation Adequate: N/A

Citation: *Rinkenberger v. City of Clearwater, MN*, (Unpub., 8th Cir. 2002)

Statute: ADA

Explanation: Federal appeals court dismissed a suit by a **Volunteer Firefighter** who was physically unable to perform his duties for 11 months. The court held that "only a permanent or long-term condition will suffice to qualify a person for the ADA's protection."

Disability: Depression

Accommodation Requested: N/A

Accommodation Required: No

Accommodation Adequate: N/A

Citation: *Bailey v. City of Englewood*, 2015 AD Cases 186121 (D. Colo. 2015)

Statute: ADA

Explanation: A **Former Firefighter/Paramedic** suffering from depression following back surgery did not have a valid claim under the ADA because he was a direct threat the public. His depression caused him to make frequent mistakes that placed those he served as a firefighter and paramedic at risk. Also, he did not offer any valid suggestions of reasonable accommodations that would assist him in performing his duties.

Disability: Headaches; Dizziness; Blackouts

Accommodation Requested: Light duty

Accommodation Required: No

Accommodation Adequate: N/A

Citation: *Beal v. Bd. of Selectmen*, 419 Mass. 535, 646 N.E.2d 131 (1995)

Statute: ADA

Explanation: A **Police Officer** at risk of blackouts in high-stress situations was deemed incapable of fulfilling the fundamental duty of protecting the public at large. The court determined that this unmanageable aspect of her condition was a great enough risk to disqualify her from the position.

Disability: Insomnia, severe migraines, depression

Accommodation Requested: Modification of work schedule

Accommodation Required: Yes

Accommodation Adequate: Maybe

Citation: *Maes v. City of Española*, 29 AD Cases 216 (D.N.M. 2014)

Statute: ADA

Explanation: Former city **Corrections Officer**, who was medically restricted from working the "graveyard" shift due to insomnia and migraine headaches, could proceed to trial with her ADA failure-to-accommodate claim based on her supervisors' refusal to excuse her from such a shift. The court noted that the officer was able to perform the essential job functions if not required to work after midnight, that supervisors were aware of her restrictions, and that City did not state a valid reason for its refusal to provide reasonable accommodation or otherwise show any undue hardship.

Disability: Narcissistic Character Disorder: Perceived

Accommodation Requested: Reconsideration of employment

Accommodation Required: No

Accommodation Adequate: N/A

Citation: *Roulette v. Human Rights Comm'n*, 256 Ill. App. 3d 682, 195 Ill. Dec. 503, 628 N.E.2d 967 (1993)

Statute: Illinois Human Rights Act, Ill. Rev. Stat. ch. 68, para. 1-101 et seq. (1991)

Explanation: A **Police Officer Applicant** was rejected employment and filed suit for disability discrimination and requested assignment. Though psychologists noted the applicant's tendency to be egotistical, superior acting, and causing difficulty in training and group environments, the court could not confirm the existence of an actionable disorder. Furthermore, even if the applicant's character traits did meet the standards of determinable mental characteristics under the statute, they would still not qualify as a protected disability because they relate directly to the employee's ability to perform the duties of the position.

Disability: Paranoid Personality Disorder

Accommodation Requested: Reinstatement or to be placed on leave until an administrative position became available

Accommodation Required: No

Accommodation Adequate: No

Citation: *Lassiter v. Reno,* 1996 U.S. App. LEXIS 13138 (4th Cir. 1996)

Statute: Rehabilitation Act

Explanation: A **US Marshal** believed that he should have been accommodated by "allowing him to return to work and regain the right to carry a weapon after periodic psychiatric evaluations" or "to transfer [him] to an administrative position in which he did not have to carry a firearm, or to place [him] on a leave of absence until an administrative position became available." However, neither were reasonable accommodations because an employee must be able to perform their job at the time during which they would have accommodations, not at some point in the future after accommodations have been provided.

Disability: Post-traumatic Stress Disorder (PTSD)

Accommodation Requested: Minimize work-related driving

Accommodation Required: Maybe

Accommodation Adequate: N/A

Citation: *Winsley v. Cook Cty.*, 563 F.3d 598 (7th Cir. 2009)

Statute: ADA

Explanation: Federal appeals court found that a P**ublic Health Nurse I** suffering from Post-Traumatic Stress Disorder that made driving difficult did not have a valid claim for accommodation under the ADA. The court found that driving was not a "major life activity" under the ADA. The court held that an inability to drive could qualify as a disability if it impaired a person from working, which is a major life activity," but that the nurse did not show that her inability to drive "significantly restricts the ability to perform a class of jobs or a broad range of jobs in various classes."

Disability: Post-traumatic Stress Disorder (PTSD)

Accommodation Requested: Reinstatement

Accommodation Required: Yes

Accommodation Adequate: Yes

Citation: *Diaz v. City of Philadelphia,* 2014 U.S. App. LEXIS 8299 (3d Cir. 2014)

Statute: ADA

Explanation: **Police Officer** had taken leave to treat a number of medical issues. Upon her return, she was accommodated by placement in the CCTV unit. After a physical altercation with a co-worker, Diaz was relocated to a patrol unit. Officer Diaz expressed concern regarding her PTSD medication and its impact on her reaction time. She was placed on "no duty" status and not provided pay or benefits. After six months of "no duty" leave Diaz failed to request further leave and did not come to work. The court held that she was reasonably accommodated by this leave as well as the opportunity to renew that leave.

Disability: Post-traumatic Stress Disorder (PTSD)

Accommodation Requested: Disability Pension

Accommodation Required: No

Accommodation Adequate: N/A

Citation: *Sullivan v. Brownlee*, 174 Ga. App. 813, 331 S.E.2d 622 (1985)

Statute: Fulton County General Employees' Pension Act

Explanation: A **Police Officer** suffering from PTSD—as diagnosed by four separate psychiatrists—following a shooting that led to her injury and the death of another officer, could not file for a disability pension. The Court found that, because two of those psychiatrists found the officer able to work in an administrative job, the availability of an equal administrative employment position was the preferred accommodation for the officer's condition.

Disability: Post-traumatic Stress Disorder (PTSD)

Accommodation Requested: Reinstatement

Accommodation Required: No

Accommodation Adequate: N/A

Citation: *Hughes v. City of Malden*, 1994 Mass. Super. LEXIS 122 (Mass. Super. Ct. 1994)

Statute: Mass. Gen. Laws ch. 151B, § 4(16)

Explanation: A **Firefighter** had a traumatic experience at the scene of a fire which led to PTSD that interfered with his work. He was ultimately deemed unfit for duty, and the department attempted to retire him involuntarily. When that failed, he was terminated. He sued for, among other things, reinstatement. However, the court held that the firefighter had offered no possible reasonable accommodation and that he was completely unqualified for the position. His termination was upheld.

Disability: Post-traumatic Stress Disorder (PTSD)

Accommodation Requested: Indoor duty

Accommodation Required: Yes

Accommodation Adequate: Yes

Citation: *Diaz v. City of Philadelphia*, 26 AD Cases 697 (E.D. Pa. 2012)

Statute: ADA

Explanation: Former **Police Officer's** accommodation request seeking restricted indoor duty, the court found, was not reasonable in view of her poor attendance record and disciplinary suspension during her prior indoor-duty assignment. The officer had been diagnosed with Post-traumatic Stress Disorder directly due to supervisor's sexual harassment. Her physician verified that she was unable to serve in any active duty role, and the court concluded that the officer was reasonably accommodated by the City with a grant of temporary unpaid leave.

Disability: Psychotic disorder

Accommodation Requested: Reinstatement

Accommodation Required: Maybe

Accommodation Adequate: Yes

Citation: *Wilson v. City of Itta Bena,* 1999 WL 1426192 (N.D. Miss. Sept. 14,1999)

Statute: ADA

Explanation: A **Police Officer** was hospitalized and diagnosed with a psychotic disorder. He was then terminated. He tried to get his job back and provided documentation of his condition. However, he did not request an accommodation until several months after he was terminated. The court held that this was too late to request an accommodation.

Disability: Stress; Anxiety; Depression

Accommodation Requested: Indefinite leave

Accommodation Required: No

Accommodation Adequate: N/A

Citation: *Davidson v. Atlantic City Police Dep't,* 1999 U.S. Dist. LEXIS 13553 (D.N.J. 1999)

Statute: ADA

Explanation: A suspended **Police Officer** requested extended sick leave to deal with psychological problems he had developed. The request was denied. The court held that demanding the employer provide indefinite leave is not reasonable. The requirements of the ADA focus on the ability of the employee to perform their job in the present with accommodation, not at some unspecified time in the future.

Disability: Unspecified mental disability

Accommodation Requested: N/A

Accommodation Required: No

Accommodation Adequate: N/A

Citation: *Pasqualetti v. Unified Gov't of Athens-Clarke Cty.*, 2015 AD Cases 192176 (M.D. Ga. 2015)

Statute: ADA

Explanation: After a line-of-duty fatal shooting, **Police Officer**'s ADA claims were denied, even though he may have shown that he was regarded as having mental impairment. The Court ruled that he did not show that the department's actions were pretext for disability bias. A former supervisor completed positive performance evaluation before shooting, psychologist found him unfit for duty, and he continued to display hostility to supervision.

Disability: Unspecified "psychological problems"

Accommodation Requested: Unclear

Accommodation Required: No

Accommodation Adequate: N/A

Citation: *Brumfield v. City of Chicago,* 735 F.3d 619 (7th Cir. 2013)

Statute: ADA; Rehabilitation Act

Explanation: A **Police Officer's** attendance and misbehavior, not a disability independent of those problems, led to their termination. "It follows that an employer need not accommodate a disability that is irrelevant to an employee's ability to perform the essential functions of her job—not because such an accommodation might be unreasonable, but because the employee is fully qualified for the job without accommodation and therefore is not entitled to an accommodation in the first place."

SUBSTANCE ABUSE

Disability: Alcoholism

Accommodation Requested: Reinstatement

Accommodation Required: No

Accommodation Adequate: Yes

Citation: *MacShane v. City of New York*, 31 AD Cases 1849 (E.D.N.Y. 2015)

Statute: ADA

Explanation: After **Police Officers** continued working on modified duty after their alcohol-related misconduct, and received individualized evaluation and diagnostic procedures, the department was entitled to summary judgment dismissing any ADA claims. The Court found that the department made a good-faith determination that officers needed treatment, and if the officers who refused, they knew the consequences of violating the orders. Additionally, the Court held that officers, who had been referred to departmental counseling unit for alcohol-abuse treatment, may not proceed with ADA retaliation claims based on their subsequent referral to counseling unit for further treatment after testifying that they had resumed drinking because it was against department policy.

Disability: Alcoholism

Accommodation Requested: Continued employment as police officer

Accommodation Required: No

Accommodation Adequate: N/A

Citation: *Antoine v. Department of Pub. Safety & Corrections,* 681 So. 2d 1282 (La. Ct. App. 1996)

Statute: ADA

Explanation: A **Policer Officer** reported for duty under the influence of alcohol, eventually blowing a .191 % BAC. The officer had been warned before about the consequences of showing up to work drunk and had been offered assistance for his drinking problem. "[T]he ADA permits an employer to terminate one under the influence of alcohol at the workplace and provides that an employer may require that employees not be under the influence of alcohol at the workplace."

Disability: Alcoholism

Accommodation Requested: Continued employment, counselling

Accommodation Required: No

Accommodation Adequate: N/A

Citation: *Rollison v. Gwinnett County,* 865 F. Supp. 1564 (N.D. Ga. 1994)

Statute: ADA; Rehabilitation Act

Explanation: **Police Officer** repeatedly engaged in fights and other negative conduct while off duty due to alcohol consumption. "While alcohol may have caused the off-duty problems, the ADA expressly provides that an employer may hold an employee to the same standards for employment or job performance as all other employees, even if the unsatisfactory performance is related to the alcoholism of the employee. …Under the ADA the employer is allowed to terminate and not accommodate an alcoholic employee, if the employee does not perform up to the same standard as all other employees, even if the behavior is related to the employee's alcoholism."

Disability: Alcoholism

Accommodation Requested: Reinstatement

Accommodation Required: No

Accommodation Adequate: Yes

Citation: *Little v. FBI,* 1 F.3d 255, 1993 U.S. App. LEXIS 20371 (4th Cir. 1993)

Statute: Rehabilitation Act

Explanation: A **FBI agent** entered an outpatient rehabilitation program after conviction for a DUI. He later relapsed while on duty and went to an inpatient program. His relapse was a violation of his probation and also constituted misconduct. He was terminated, stating he had recovered. The FBI had already permitted him to go to rehab and was permitted to fire him.

Disability: Alcoholism

Accommodation Requested: Continued employment as police officer

Accommodation Required: No **Accommodation Adequate:** N/A

Citation: *Shields v. City of Shreveport*, 579 So. 2d 961 (La. Ct. App. 1991) **Statute:** Rehabilitation Act

Explanation: Two **Police Officers** were dismissed after consuming alcohol on duty while providing security during a high school reunion. They were determined to be alcoholics, but the court upheld their termination as based not on their alcoholism but their misconduct and the fact that they broke numerous rules throughout the event. "It appears from the plain language of the statute that only alcoholics . . . whose problems are under control are protected from discriminatory treatment."

Disability: Alcoholism

Accommodation Requested: Overturning termination for DUI arrest

Accommodation Required: Maybe **Accommodation Adequate:** N/A

Citation: *Budde v. Kane Cty. Forest Pres.*, 603 F. Supp. 2d 1136 (N.D. Ill. 2009) **Statute:** ADA

Explanation: **Former Police Chief** could not request reasonable accommodation for alcoholism under the ADA in relation to the violation of a universally applicable work rule (here a rule subjecting employees to discipline for the violation of any Federal, State, County, or Municipal law). The court held that though the employee's disability was a partial cause of his arrest for DUI, it was not the only one (E.g. his decision to drive while intoxicated). Therefore, while there were multiple contributing factors for his violation of the work rule, the violation of the rule was the sole cause of his termination.

Disability: Alcoholism

Accommodation Requested: EAP Monitoring

Accommodation Required: No **Accommodation Adequate:** N/A

Citation: *Brennan v. NYC Police Dept.*, (Unpub. 2nd Cir. 1998) **Statute:** ADA

Explanation: The fact that the **Police Officer** was a recovering alcoholic does not excuse their losing an issued firearm while sleeping on a subway train.

Disability: Alcoholism

Accommodation Requested: Not putting employee in a position where he would be required to drive, pairing employee with others who could drive.

Accommodation Required: No

Accommodation Adequate: N/A

Citation: *Sizemore v. Dep't of Rehab. & Corr.*, 63 Ohio Misc. 2d 319, 629 N.E.2d 1096 (Ct. Cl. 1992)
http://www.testclear.com/court_cases/cases/New-York-THOMAS-BRENNAN,-Plaintiff-Appellant,-vs-NEW-YORK-CITY-POLICE-DEPARTMENT--as-Successor-in-interest-to-NYC-Transit-Police-Department,--WILLIAM-BRATTON,-Commissioner,-NEW-YORK-CITY-TRANSIT-POLICE,-MICHAEL-OCONNOR.aspx

Statute: Ohio Rev. Code Ann. § 4112.02

Explanation: A **Corrections Officer** charged with 11 DUI's was found to have no right to reasonable accommodation. The court held that the officer's request would unduly burden the employer, and that it would incur additional liability if employee were ever required to drive in emergency circumstances.

Disability: Alcoholism

Accommodation Requested: Policies

Accommodation Required: Maybe

Accommodation Adequate: Yes

Citation: *Knowles v. Sheriff*, 460 Fed. Appx. 833 (11th Cir. 2012)

Statute: ADA

Explanation: Alcoholic former **Deputy Sheriff's** failure-to-accommodate claim was dismissed, despite his allegation that he would have voluntarily sought employee assistance program treatment if not for "communication breakdown" as to whether he was to be directed to enter a program. Such a communication breakdown, the court ruled, was not evidence of bad faith or unwillingness to accommodate on the part of the sheriff's office.

Disability: Alcoholism

Accommodation Requested: Treatment for Alcoholism in lieu of termination

Accommodation Required: No

Accommodation Adequate: N/A

Citation: *Butler v. Thornburgh*, 900 F.2d 871 (5th Cir. 1990)

Statute: Rehabilitation Act

Explanation: An alcoholic **FBI Agent** was denied accommodation to treat his disease instead of being terminated because the court found that his four previous alcohol-related disruptions (drunkenly instigating a fight, crashing an agency vehicle while drunk, etc.) at work disqualified him as an agent.

Disability: Alcoholism

Accommodation Requested: Treatment for Alcoholism in lieu of termination

Accommodation Required: No **Accommodation Adequate:** N/A

Citation: *Butler v. Thornburgh*, 900 F.2d 871 (5th Cir. 1990) **Statute:** Rehabilitation Act

Explanation: An alcoholic **Criminal Investigator** for the ATF was denied accommodation to treat his disease instead of being terminated because the court found that his commission of vehicular homicide, not the associated alcoholism, was the cause of discharge. That conduct disqualified him from service.

Disability: Alcoholism

Accommodation Requested: Reinstatement

Accommodation Required: No **Accommodation Adequate:** Yes

Citation: *Maull v. Div. of State Police,* 141 F. Supp. 2d 463 (D. Del. 2001) **Statute:** ADA

Explanation: The employer had granted a **State Trooper** leave to complete a treatment program, but was still justified in terminating him due to the risk he posed to the public's safety. He had engaged in extensive misconduct, and even though much of it stemmed from his alcoholism, the department wasn't required to tolerate this behavior. Furthermore, they were not required to monitor an alcoholic officer to ensure he was prepared to respond to calls at any time.

Disability: Alcoholism

Accommodation Requested: Reassignment to position closer to his treatment facility, rearrange schedule to facilitate treatment

Accommodation Required: No **Accommodation Adequate:** N/A

Citation: *Roberts v. New York State Dep't of Correctional Servs.,* 63 F. Supp. 2d 272 (W.D.N.Y. 1999) **Statute:** ADA

Explanation: Employers are not required to provide accommodation for employees whose lives are not impaired by their illness, as that fails to rise to the status of a disability requiring accommodation. In this case, a **Corrections Officer** wanted to either be transferred to a facility closer to where he received treatment for his alcoholism or rearrange his schedule to make travelling 60 miles to treatment less burdensome. However, employers don't need to make a situation less burdensome when the alcoholism doesn't rise to the level of a disability.

Disability: Alcoholism; Depression

Accommodation Requested: Transfer to another facility within the department of corrections

Accommodation Required: No

Accommodation Adequate: N/A

Citation: *Wallin v. Minnesota Dep't of Corrections,* 974 F. Supp. 1234 (D. Minn. 1997)

Statute: ADA

Explanation: A **Corrections Officer** was almost discharged for attacking his girlfriend, but instead was required to complete a treatment program and stay chemical-free for three years. He had problems with his coworkers after his return, and held that he was mistreated based on his disability and requested a transfer to accommodate his condition. The court stated that transfer to another facility would not have accommodated the employee's specific disability; he still would have performed the same duties as he had before. A transfer would therefore not have been a reasonable accommodation.

Disability: Alcoholism; Drug use

Accommodation Requested: Continued employment

Accommodation Required: Yes

Accommodation Adequate: Yes

Citation: *Van Ever v. New York State Dep't of Correctional Servs.,* 2000 U.S. Dist. LEXIS 16960 (S.D.N.Y. 2000)

Statute: ADA

Explanation: A **Corrections Officer** was terminated for his abuse of alcohol and mood-altering substances. He requested continued employment that accommodated rehabilitative treatment. "Alcoholism is not a per se disability under the ADA," but employers can provide unpaid leave in order to enter a treatment program. Here, the employer provided the employee with three leaves of absence to complete rehabilitation programs. When the employee continued to have issues the employer was not required to do more than they already had and were permitted to let the employee go.

Disability: Alcoholism; Drug use

Accommodation Requested: Continued employment

Accommodation Required: Maybe

Accommodation Adequate: N/A

Citation: *Green v. Pike Rd. Volunteer Fire Prot. Auth.*, Civil Action No. 2:15cv253-WHA, 2016 U.S. Dist. (M.D. Ala. June 1, 2016)

Statute: ADA

Explanation: A **Firefighter** terminated for failing to notify the department of a DUI might be granted a right to reasonable accommodation under the ADA if he can show comments by his supervisors about his past drug and alcohol use show that his drug and alcohol problems were the true motivation behind his termination.

Disability: Drug addiction

Accommodation Requested: Reinstatement

Accommodation Required: No

Accommodation Adequate: N/A

Citation: *Desper v. Montgomery County,* 727 F. Supp. 959 (E.D. Pa. 1990)

Statute: Rehabilitation Act

Explanation: A police department was not required to accommodate a **Narcotics Officer** who was addicted to drugs. As a drug user he was not qualified for the position. Accommodating him in that particular program would not have been reasonable.

MISCELLANEOUS DISORDERS AND DISEASES

Disability: Brain Tumor

Accommodation Requested: Return to duty

Accommodation Required: No

Accommodation Adequate: N/A

Citation: *Michael v. City of Troy Police Dep't*, 32 AD Cases 744 (6th Cir. 2015)

Statute: ADA

Explanation: After a **Police Officer** was diagnosed with a brain tumor and found unfit for duty by two physicians, the City of Troy was entitled to summary judgment dismissing his ADA claims even though his medical witnesses concluded that he could return to work. The City could rely on physicians' objectively reasonable opinions that officer posed direct safety threat to himself and others based extensive assessments of officer's ability to perform police duties.

Disability: Bleeding from nose and mouth every time exposed to smoke

Accommodation Requested: Transfer to another position

Accommodation Required: No

Accommodation Adequate: N/A

Citation: *Ramie v. Department of Fire*, 617 So. 2d 92, (La. Ct. App. 1993)

Statute: La. R.S. 46:2254

Explanation: After he was terminated because he was unable to fight fires, a **Firefighter** claimed the department had failed to accommodate him when he was not transferred to another position in the fire suppression division or another job with the city. The court upheld his termination and stated that the department had not failed to accommodate him. Everyone in the fire suppression division needed to be able to fight fires and those in charge of the department did not have the authority to transfer him elsewhere in the city. Furthermore, there were no other positions available in the department when he was terminated.

Disability: Cancer

Accommodation Requested: Assignment to vacant lieutenant position

Accommodation Required: No

Accommodation Adequate: N/A

Citation: *Spears v. Creel*, 31 AD Cases 832 (11th Cir. Ct. App. 2015)

Statute: ADA, FMLA

Explanation: Sheriff was not required to accommodate a **Corrections Lieutenant** who was terminated while being treated for cancer because no lieutenant positions were available, her entire unit had been discontinued, and she did not request a reasonable accommodation.

Disability: Cancer: Breast Cancer

Accommodation Requested: Reinstatement with full back pay

Accommodation Required: No

Accommodation Adequate: Yes

Citation: *Wilson v. Gaston County*, 2015 AD Cases 367569 (W.D.N.C. 2015)

Statute: ADA

Explanation: County **Paramedic**, temporarily discharged after she requested leave for potential breast cancer surgery, brought discrimination and retaliation claims against Gaston County. The court rejected the paramedic's claims where she failed to show that her termination for multiple moving violations that prevented her from driving ambulance was discriminatory. In addition, the court held that the fact that she received more frequent written warnings than her co-workers for similar misconduct was not sufficient to show retaliation.

Disability: Cancer: Breast Cancer

Accommodation Requested: Leave of absence

Accommodation Required: Yes

Accommodation Adequate: Yes

Citation: *Moore v. Maryland Dep't of Public Safety & Correctional Services,* 27 AD Cases 849 (D. Md. 2013)

Statute: Rehabilitation Act

Explanation: State prison **Corrections Officer**, who was placed on unpaid medical leave during treatment for breast cancer, could not proceed with a failure-to-accommodate claim. The officer had been granted eight-month leave, despite state law requiring payroll separation after six months. She repeatedly stated that she did not know when she could return to work; her request for another leave extension was determined by the court to not be reasonable. It also noted that she had reinstated at new location without reduction in pay or grade.

Disability: Chronic Fatigue Syndrome

Accommodation Requested: Transfer to courthouse position

Accommodation Required: Yes

Accommodation Adequate: No

Citation: *Woodson v. Cook County Sheriff,* 1996 U.S. Dist. LEXIS 15475 (N.D. Ill. 1996)

Statute: ADA

Explanation: Instead of providing a **Deputy Sheriff** with her requested transfer or any other alternative, the employer increased the employee's workload until she resigned. The employee was permitted to continue to trial on her failure to accommodate claim.

Disability: Chronic Fatigue Syndrome; Fibromyalgia

Accommodation Requested: Permanent assignment to day shift

Accommodation Required: Maybe

Accommodation Adequate: N/A

Citation: *Holt v. Olmsted Twp. Bd. of Trustees,* 43 F. Supp. 2d 812 (N.D. Ohio 1998)

Statute: ADA

Explanation: A **Dispatcher** with numerous health issues requested accommodation in the form of consistent shift assignments. The employer provided these for a while, but became concerned about the feelings of the other employees and ceased the accommodation. The court held that a permanent assignment to the day shift may not be an undue hardship for the employer just because other employees will be disgruntled that they will be forced to work less desired shifts. The employer has to prove more than disapproval by other employees.

Disability: Crohn's Disease; Necrosis of the tibias in both legs resulting from treatment

Accommodation Requested: Light duty

Accommodation Required: No **Accommodation Adequate:** Yes

Citation: *Hardy v. Village of Piermont,* 923 F. Supp. 604 (S.D.N.Y. 1996) **Statute:** Rehabilitation Act

Explanation: A **Police Officer** unable to walk or run wanted to be provided a light duty position, but none existed in the department so she was placed on medical leave when her sick leave ran out. The court held that this was a reasonable accommodation because the employer was not obligated to create a light duty position for the employee.

Disability: Fibromyalgia

Accommodation Requested: Reinstatement

Accommodation Required: No **Accommodation Adequate:** Yes

Citation: *Jackson v. City of Chicago,* 293 F. Supp. 2d 836 (N.D. Ill. 2003) **Statute:** ADA

Explanation: The city was not required to reinstate a **Police Officer** who could not safely use a gun and often had trouble standing and would collapse. The employee then stated that she had not been accommodated by being informed of potential reassignments. However, the city had informed her repeatedly of opportunities and she had failed to avail herself of these opportunities. The officer did not engage in reassignment procedures and was therefore the party at fault.

Disability: Fibromyalgia

Accommodation Requested: Elimination of a lifting requirement of 40 pounds

Accommodation Required: No **Accommodation Adequate:** N/A

Citation: *Scruggs v. Pulaski Cnty.*, 817 F.3d 1087 (8th Cir. 2016) **Statute:** ADA; Rehabilitation Act

Explanation: A **Juvenile Detention Officer** was rightfully denied an accommodation removing the 40 pound lifting requirement demanded of all officers in her position. The requirement was found by the court to be necessary to the essential function of the position, which is to maintain order among juveniles, all of which were at least 40 pounds.

Disability: Hearing Disability: Impaired hearing in left ear

Accommodation Requested: Continued employment as police officer

Accommodation Required: Yes

Accommodation Adequate: Yes

Citation: *Karbusicky v. City of Park Ridge,* 950 F. Supp. 878 (N.D. Ill. 1997)

Statute: ADA

Explanation: **Police Officer** had very poor hearing in one ear which led to difficulty performing his duties. He was offered a series of accommodations, including a hearing aid, before he was transferred to a Community Service Officer position. "While reassignment is to be considered only after other accommodations within the employee's current position are attempted...defendant has made such attempts in the instant case by providing or offering to provide hearing aids that plaintiff regards as ineffective. Plaintiff has suggested no other method of accommodation that he could be offered in light of the fact...that plaintiff cannot perform the essential functions of a police officer.... Based on these uncontested facts, the court finds that defendant's decision to reassign plaintiff to the position of CSO is a reasonable accommodation as a matter of law."

Disability: Hearing Disability

Accommodation Requested: Amplification system or physical ques while on firing line

Accommodation Required: Maybe

Accommodation Adequate: Maybe

Citation: *Packard v. Gordon*, 148 Vt. 579, 537 A.2d 140 (1987)

Statute: Vermont Fair Employment Practices Act

Explanation: A **"Call" Firefighter** had a "significant hearing problem" and could not understand some instructions during firing exercises. Court determined that a jury could find the requested accommodations reasonable, and remanded back to trial court.

Disability: Hearing Disability: bilateral mild to moderately severe sensorineural hearing loss

Accommodation Requested: Use of hearing aids

Accommodation Required: No

Accommodation Adequate: N/A

Citation: *Carleton v. Commonwealth*, 447 Mass. 791, 858 N.E.2d 258 (2006)

Statute: ADA

Explanation: Court held that hearing aids were not a reasonable accommodation for a hearing-impaired **Firefighter**.

Disability: HIV/AIDS

Accommodation Requested: Unclear

Accommodation Required: Yes
Accommodation Adequate: Yes

Citation: *Severino v. North Ft. Myers Fire Control Dist.,* 935 F.2d 1179 (11th Cir. 1991)
Statute: Rehabilitation Act

Explanation: After being diagnosed with HIV/AIDS a **Firefighter** willingly resigned. He was offered "light duty" but complained about the responsibilities he was given, calling them "demeaning." He became confrontational about his position and was fired after he refused to perform his duties. The employer had made reasonable accommodations and upheld the employee's termination for his behavior.

Disability: Incontinence

Accommodation Requested: Work specific shifts

Accommodation Required: Yes
Accommodation Adequate: Yes

Citation: *Andrews v. Virginia,* 2000 U.S. App. LEXIS 24264 (4th Cir. 2000)
Statute: ADA

Explanation: Employees are not permitted to limit what accommodations they are provided by employers. Here, the **Corrections Officer** was offered multiple options of accommodations. When she picked one and it did not work out, she was not entitled to demand a specific type of accommodation that she preferred.

Disability: Pseudo folliculitis barbae (PFB)

Accommodation Requested: To be free from clean-shaven requirement

Accommodation Required: No
Accommodation Adequate: N/A

Citation: *Fitzpatrick v. City of Atlanta,* 2 F.3d 1112 (11th Cir. 1993)
Statute: ADA; Rehabilitation Act

Explanation: The fire department implemented a policy requiring all **Firefighters** to be clean shaven in order to ensure that their SCBA gear was properly sealed to their faces. A number of firefighters struggled with PFB, which prevented them from being clean shaven. The court upheld the policy based on the necessity of a proper SCBA seal to the face and the fact that the firefighters challenging the policy provided no reasonable alternative to the requirement.

Disability: Sarcoidosis

Accommodation Requested: Remaining on light duty assignment

Accommodation Required: Yes
Accommodation Adequate: No

Citation: *Allen v. Baltimore County,* 31
Statute: ADA

AD Cases 709 (D. Md. 2015)

Explanation: A **Corrections Officer** was demoted after he was physically impaired by his inflammatory disease. The officer claimed that he had been unlawfully demoted in violation of the ADA because of his impairment, and could be reasonably accommodated by light duty assignments and being allowed to take his medication. The trial court agreed, finding that he was qualified under the ADA and his employer failed to accommodate him, and allowed his case to go to trial.

Disability: Sleeping Problems: Obstructive Sleep Apnea

Accommodation Requested: Day shift Schedule

Accommodation Required: Yes

Accommodation Adequate: Yes

Citation: *Herr v. City of Chi.*, 479 F. Supp. 2d 834 (N.D. Ill. 2007)

Statute: ADA

Explanation: A **Criminal History Analyst** who refused employer's offer of reasonable accommodation could not then hold that employer liable for failing to reasonably accommodate. An employer is not required to accommodate disabled employees if doing so affects the collectively bargained rights of other employees.

Disability: Sleeping Problems: Sleep Apnea

Accommodation Requested: Assignment to only day shifts, while keeping an independent one-evening-a-week teaching position

Accommodation Required: Yes

Accommodation Adequate: No

Citation: *Silk v. City of Chi.*, 194 F.3d 788 (7th Cir. 1999)

Statute: ADA, Rehabilitation Act

Explanation: Court held that a **Police Officer** granted day shifts in accommodation of his sleep apnea was not permitted to continue teaching a class one evening a week because department policy stated clearly that employees on limited duty may not engage in secondary employment inconsistent with their limitations. A night shift of any kind is inconsistent with a request for accommodation of assignment to only day shifts.

Disability: Sleeping Problems: Delayed Sleep Phase Syndrome; Sleep Apnea

Accommodation Requested: Adjusting work schedule from beginning at 9:00 a.m. to beginning at 11:00 a.m.

Accommodation Required: Maybe

Accommodation Adequate: N/A

Citation: *Kendall v. Ashcroft*, EEOC Petition No. 03A50006, MSPB No. SF-

Statute: Rehabilitation Act

0752-04-0153-I-2

Explanation: The Merit Systems Protection Board found that an **Intelligence Research Specialist**'s accommodation request to push the start of his shift two hours later was not reasonable because his past behavior of being *more* than two hours late implied that the accommodation would not be effective. The court found that the only effective accommodation would have been to allow the employee to work whenever he was able, which was inherently unreasonable. An accommodation cannot be reasonable if it is ineffective, but just because an accommodation is effective does not mean it is reasonable.

Disability: Not Stated

Accommodation Requested: Sick leave and wage continuation

Accommodation Required: No

Accommodation Adequate: Yes

Citation: *Gardner v. Sch. Dist. of Phila.*, 32 AD Cases 738 (3d Cir. 2015)

Statute: ADA

Explanation: After former **School Police Officer** never returned to work following sick leave for an injury suffered while on the job, the officer lost his status as a "qualified individual" under the ADA. An inability to be physically present at school rendered him unqualified for the position.

Disability: Not Stated

Accommodation Requested: Reinstatement

Accommodation Required: No

Accommodation Adequate: N/A

Citation: *Moore v. Mancuso*, 2015 AD Cases 366729 (W.D. La. 2015)

Statute: ADA

Explanation: Injured former **Sheriff's Deputy** may not proceed with ADA failure-to-accommodate claim based on his transfer and then discharge after investigation of his sexual harassment of co-worker. The court found that the deputy did not afford the sheriff an opportunity to provide accommodation given that he was absent on sick leave from his date of transfer until his discharge. Further, the supervisor's meeting to discuss the deputy's limitations demonstrated a willingness to engage in an interactive process and a history of prior accommodations contradicted the allegation that the reason for his discharge was pretextual.

Disability: Not Stated

Accommodation Requested: Reinstatement

Accommodation Required: No

Accommodation Adequate: N/A

Citation: *Adair v. City of Muskogee*, 2015 AD Cases 192642 (E.D. Okla. 2015)

Statute: ADA

Explanation: After a **Former Firefighter** was given lifting restrictions due to a work-related injury, he raised claims under the ADA for a constructive discharge claim based on his disability retirement in lieu of discharge, and for a claim that the medical examination he underwent violated the ADA. The Court held that he may not proceed with ADA claims because his inability to perform firefighter job is insufficient to show that he was precluded from performing broad class or range of jobs, and his claim against the medical examination was not viable because voluntary medical examination in connection with pursuit of such a claim is job-related and consistent with business necessity.

Disability: Not Stated

Accommodation Requested: Reassignment

Accommodation Required: Yes

Accommodation Adequate: No

Citation: *Davoll v. Webb*, 194 F.3d 1116 (10th Cir. 1999); prior decis. at 49 F. Supp. 2d 1233 (D. Colo. 1997)

Statute: ADA

Explanation: After **Former Police Officers** were injured in the line of duty and forced to retire due to Denver's policy forbidding disabled police officers from transferring into other vacant positions in the city government, the district court properly refused an interpretation of the ADA that simply requires equal treatment of disabled and non-disabled employees. An employer's policy that does not provide accommodations for non-disabled employees does not excuse employer's failure to accommodate disabled employees.

Disability: Not Stated

Accommodation Requested: Reassignment

Accommodation Required: Yes

Accommodation Adequate: No

Citation: *United States v. City & County of Denver,* 943 F. Supp. 1304 (D. Colo. 1996)

Statute: ADA

Explanation: **Police Officers** were placed in limited duty after being injured with instructions to apply for disability retirement. They sued because the department refused to reassign them. The city countered that reassignment would be an undue hardship on them. The court "stated the term included "an individual with a disability, who, with or without reasonable accommodation, can perform the essential functions of the employment position that such individual holds or desires" and "reasonable accommodation" may include "reassignment to a vacant position." These positions could include "a non-patrol vacant position, not having as an essential function, the power to make a forcible arrest or fire a weapon."

Disability: Not Stated

Accommodation Requested: Transfer to positions that do not have contact with prison inmates

Accommodation Required: Maybe

Accommodation Adequate: N/A

Citation: *Sharp v. Abate*, 887 F. Supp. 695 (S.D.N.Y. 1995)

Statute: ADA

Explanation: Court acknowledged that due to the existence of numerous sub-positions that lack any inmate contact, contact with inmates might not be an essential function of the job of **Corrections Officer**.

Disability: Not Stated

Accommodation Requested: Permanent light-duty assignments

Accommodation Required: No

Accommodation Adequate: N/A

Citation: *Matos v. City of Phx.*, 176 Ariz. 125, 859 P.2d 748 (Ct. App. 1993)

Statute: Arizona Civil Rights Act, Ariz. Stat. Rev. §§ 41-1461

Explanation: Disabled **Police Officers** who had been transferred to temporary light-duty positions to accommodate their limitations were denied a request to make those positions permanent. An employer is not required to create new roles to accommodate disabled employees, and temporary positions do not qualify as established roles that may be used as permanent accommodations.

Disability: Not stated

Accommodation Requested: Permanent assignment to light-duty position

Accommodation Required: No

Accommodation Adequate: N/A

Citation: *Fasone v. Clinton Twp.*, 1998 U.S. App. LEXIS 7070 (6th Cir. 1998)

Statute: ADA

Explanation: A **Firefighter** incapable of fighting fires requested assignment to the position of Fire Prevention Officer. However, there was no vacant fire prevention position. The employer would have had to create a new position for the employee. The court held that the employer was not obligated to create a new position to accommodate the firefighter, as that would be unreasonable.

Disability: Not Stated

Accommodation Requested: Permanent light duty, administrative work only

Accommodation Required: Yes

Accommodation Adequate: Yes

Citation: *Cuiellette v. City of Los Angeles*, 194 Cal. App. 4th 757, 123 Cal.Rptr.3d 562 (2011)

Statute: FEHA

Explanation: A California appeals court held that a **Police Officer's** 100% total permanent disability rating received during a worker's compensation proceeding following his removal from full-duty work could not be used as justification of his subsequent termination from a permanent light-duty position.

Disability: Not Stated: including passing out

Accommodation Requested: Reassignment/light duty

Accommodation Required: Yes

Accommodation Adequate: No

Citation: *Gilbert v. City of St. Charles*, 1999 U.S. Dist. LEXIS 4095 (N.D. Ill. 1999)

Statute: ADA

Explanation: A **Police Officer** provided his employer with a note on his doctor's prescription pad requesting light duty, though the officer himself never specifically requested accommodation. An employee does not have to clamor aggressively in requesting an accommodation, the employer needs to meet the employee halfway. It has to see if any light duty positions are available. Furthermore, "[w]hile the City was not required to indefinitely "provide a job, but not require that [he] regularly perform it," it was required to engage in an interactive process to determine whether Gilbert was entitled to a medical leave and, if so, the conditions and length of the leave."

Disability: Not Stated

Accommodation Requested: Transition of light duty positions from temporary to permanent

Accommodation Required: No

Accommodation Adequate: N/A

Citation: Allen v. Hamm, 2006 U.S. Dist. LEXIS 6707, 17 Am. Disabilities Cas. (BNA) 1206 (D. Md. Feb. 22, 2006)

Statute: ADA, Rehabilitation Act

Explanation: **Police Officers** could not request accommodation that eliminated the essential functions of their jobs. A permanent light duty position effectively eliminates essential functions—making a forcible arrest, emergency operation of a vehicle, firing a weapon—of an officer's duty, and thus is an unreasonable accommodation.

Disability: Not Stated

Accommodation Requested: Light-duty position, shifting some duties to other employees

Accommodation Required: Yes

Accommodation Adequate: Yes

Citation: *Hoskins v. Oakland County Sheriff's Dep't,* 227 F.3d 719 (6th Cir. 2000)

Statute: ADA

Explanation: A **Deputy Sheriff** was seriously injured outside of work, resulting in limitations in her ability to lift objects and requiring she be kept away from situations where she could be hit in the chest. However, there were no light duty positions available and she was terminated. The employer is not required to accommodate an employee by putting the responsibility for an essential job function on another employer. "[T]he ADA does not require employers to accommodate individuals by shifting an essential job function onto others." Furthermore, making a temporary light-duty position permanent is the equivalent of creating a new position, which the employer is not required to do.

Made in the USA
Monee, IL
05 November 2026

67378970R00103